SIGNATURE PAGE

A STROKE OF RECOVERY

PART 2: RECOVERY CONTINUES

MEETRI'A ANGELO

DEDICATION

I want to dedicate this piece of work to a group of people that have been my army consistently for several years. To my social media friends, fans, cheerleaders and support system. You all have been on so many journeys with me and helped me in ways that I could not put into words. Thank you for keeping me, keeping you going.

Meetri'a Angelo

INTRODUCTION

As I finished my first book '*A Stroke Of Recovery*', I felt that I had achieved a huge milestone. I had suffered a massive and dense stroke and I had recovered - not to my baseline - but to a place where I could live independently again. A milestone that many aren't fortunate enough to reach. A whole new recovery was looming ahead of me and I had a feeling that it would be just as important to document. I had reached a milestone, but not the finish line. I actually realized that the finish line was much further away. I even considered that the finish line may not exist at all. I finished my first book in October of 2023 and I started working on the publishing. I hoped that my life was going to get much better. It seemed inevitable. So many things seemed to be going in the right direction. At a time of great hope and optimism, I was informed that my Medicaid coverage would be ending their payments to the nursing home that December. I was still waiting for my disability to be approved, with no timeline in sight and no place to go. At the time, most people had either stopped coming to see me or they never really came to see me in the first place. I felt cut off from the world and I wasn't sure of my exact plans. I did know that without my independence, I was going to feel like a burden.

I continued tracking my experiences since the end of the first book. I just imagined that if people found the first book interesting at all, they might like what follows. If there is one thing in my life that I could rely on, wild shit always happened to me. I always joked that I should have my own reality show. I figured wild shit would definitely come up as I experienced my new way of living. Luckily, I already developed the mindset that I would be learning a new normal. The idea of returning to my previous '*normal*' was a wish, but not the ultimate goal. I was prepared to make changes in my daily living and I just wanted to get back to a more independent lifestyle. This is what both excited and terrified me. In all honesty, I still struggle with this. The worry that my independence could cause me great harm or death, while also wanting my independence more than anything in the world. I am working through it in therapy. More about that later. This will not only be an extension of my first book, but a look at the growth I've been making and how significant changes in your life can be viewed as a damaging negative or you can rewrite them into a positive. I wrote about grief, growing up with trauma, but underneath everything, I wrote about growth and improvement. In the nursing home I was in therapy to improve my body. However, I was left on my own to improve my mental health. In certain cases, I was forced to learn to not only cope with these crises, but I was also forced to learn to process these emotions in a healthy way. All of my amateur Google searches for information on how to process these emotions turned out helpful. I had to do something to alleviate these emotions that were crippling me. Writing the things down that are bothering you was a recommended way to get these feelings out of your system. I was used to keeping random notebooks around so that I could write. I actually published most of those thoughts in my first book. In this installment, I will be focusing on even more mental health growth. I considered myself a strong person before claiming my truth as transgender. Claiming a truth that I knew could cost me everything, made me even stronger. Seeing that I could survive something like my stroke, I began feeling that I am nearly unbreakable, but not without some help. Counseling and therapy opened my eyes so much. So much so, that I'm now working towards my own license to help others the way it helped me. Follow me on the second part of my journey. I hope it helps you and I hope you find the hope, joy, strength or whatever positive influence you need to keep pushing through.

THE END OF A CHAPTER

When last we left her, Meetri'a had been begging for a discharge date from day one of her stroke. If I haven't made it clear, I had asked about my discharge date at least a thousand times since the day I had the stroke. I was always left disappointed after asking. I kept getting told that my recovery was up to me. What the hell was I supposed to do with this incredibly ominous message? It also felt like I was failing my recovery if I wasn't discharged before my life fell apart. It was like I could hear the doomsday clock ticking as I waited for my apartment complex to evict me and my credit to be annihilated. It felt like there was no stopping it. I was trapped. Everyday was like I was chained to my bed and

I was being taunted by life. I assumed a discharge date is what I needed to start recovering. I wanted a goal to work towards. I realize now, that I had it backwards. I needed to start healing in order to be discharged. I assumed that I would just be waiting for my brain to do its own thing. Once I finally understood that I needed to help it along, we seemed to make a lot of progress in my recovery, quickly. With the recovery that I had made, that discharge day was finally coming. I kept a diary after my first book was complete. I will be adding some of those entries in this book.

November 15, 2023

Life is going to come at me very quickly in the next few weeks and my nerves and anxiety are trying to get the better of me. I have to leave the nursing home by December 3rd and it's a good thing because I've recovered enough to no longer need medically assisted living, but I don't have any income or any solid place to go. I haven't had any money since my last unemployment payment in January right before my stroke. So with no income, no job, no option to work a normal 9 to 5 and no savings, how am I supposed to find housing? I moved into this temporary home on Valentine's day and I haven't been happy living here, but I am scared about what awaits me outside of these walls. I'm vocal, so I've discussed this with my social worker. She tells me constantly about all of these programs that are available but I'm still waiting to hear from some that I applied to in February when I first got here. Others have flat out told me that they can't help. They said I need to be in a homeless shelter or sleeping in a park for them to even acknowledge that you may need help. I'm learning that our system in this country is so reactive when being proactive could change so many things. The problem with bing proactive is that people think you are scamming the system. While being reactive causes more people to become statistics in the system. Our system offers so many opportunities, but discourages it be used. When you use them it's like a red mark on your 'permanent record'. One of my first thoughts was how society will judge me for using social programs, even when I need them. If it truly didn't matter, why would they ask you if you've received benefits previously. That question is one of those discriminating "nondiscriminatory" questions, like disclosing your ethnicity, race, or maiden name. Having worked as a manager that dealt with application selection and also having worked in recruitment, You learn to read between the lines of a resume or an application. Either way, what does my asking for help to survive in this world have to do with my ability to work for you and make your business money? I don't believe it matters, but should I ever need to seek a normal 9 to 5 again, that is something I will get to be judged on. I'll cross that bridge when I need to.

I had dreamed of the day I finally went home. The day was scheduled, but I had no home to go to. I remember the anxiety. I had no solid plan, but I had concepts of a plan. (Insert eye roll here). However, I was just waiting for a few things to fall in place. I just needed to have a good sleep and have faith that the universe was going to have my back. When I needed it most the universe came through. The universe is balanced and I needed that.

November 16, 2023

BIG NEWS! I finally got approved for my disability! It took almost 11 months! The relief I feel is unparalleled to the good feelings I've had so far during this recovery. This means I'm going to have the ability to actually rebuild. I'll actually have a shot. I was told that many people are denied disability, not only the first time but multiple times. I was sure I had the time to be denied repeatedly. As the days continued to go by, my anxiety intensified. Life requires money. I haven't had any since before this stroke. My optimism of the future is suddenly abundant and I feel so full. I sent my first manuscript out today for review. The reaction to it thus far has been very promising. I truly feel the winds of change in the air. I've already been denied once for new housing thanks to my eviction which was entirely beyond my control. Everything is so black and white to these automated systems. I need a human to empathize with my situation. Not many consider the gray area anymore. Sure I have an eviction, but it was while I was confined to a hospital bed. Is there any leniency? I just need a chance. A chan-

ce to rebuild, a chance to survive. Sometimes we have to create our own chances though, don't we? Sometimes it can get us in trouble but if we do it right we can make huge differences. That's my goal. I want to make a difference. I tried the pre-paved paths and they didn't work for me. I needed to create my own. My own paths and my own chances. I want to make a difference. Not just for me, but also for others too. The holidays are approaching fast, but this whole year was fast to me. Time flies when you're laying in a hospital bed. It also went by at a snail's pace. It's hard to explain. I will get out of here around the beginning of December. My chosen family has plans with me to take me out of the nursing home for Thanksgiving. I don't typically like Thanksgiving. It was always filled with people being disappointed in the meal or people yelling. You know, time with family. Maybe not all families are like that, but my family was. I enjoy the vibes of the holiday season. It seems like there is so much magic in the air. It's beautiful. Most worries seem to melt away. The magic created in the movies or the music seems to materialize. We are all swallowed by nostalgia then spit out by harsh reality. It's disheartening but for a while we can all disconnect and just live in the magic of the holidays. The energy is so strong. The atmosphere can change your whole attitude. Is it permanent? No! However, it is good in the moment. This next week, I'll get to experience that magic with people that I love. Shortly after that I'll enter the real world, again. The problems of the real world will return too. That has been a benefit to this experience, in a way. I was able to be removed from the real world and all of its problems and that was kind of nice. I had other problems obviously, but I didn't have to stress myself out with the same problems I had been dealing with before my stroke. No rogue or forgotten bills in the mail. No being late for work, no work reprimands for stupid shit. No work at all. Soon, those problems will return, and they will work in tandem with my new problems to cause issues. Maybe not the exact same, but very similar. I'm supposed to hear back from my publishers in 3-6 days. I'm throwing every good vibe at it and I am manifesting great news.

My holiday season was due to kick off with a great

boost to my confidence. My disability was finally approved my life was about to restart and with it, a good chance to succeed. A chapter that I had been struggling through, was finally closing and a new chapter was starting. It's funny because looking back at everything it literally felt the page of a book being turned. At the time it's all so real. When I was writing my first book, everything seemed surreal. Everyday, I relived my lasts. My last weekend out, my last day spent with my dog and my last morning I woke up "*normal*". I was going to feel some normalcy again very soon.

In my journal entry I talk about how my chosen family planned on taking me out of the nursing home. My mother contacted me about coming over for their thanksgiving, too. Here was the difference. My mother asked WHEN I would be coming over. My chosen family asked me what I needed in order for me to come over for thanksgiving. My own mother, the woman experiencing her own medical issues that came along with her own physical limitations, was talking to her daughter, who just had a stroke and simply wanted to know when I would be over for Thanksgiving. She wouldn't have had to ask if she had ever come to see me. I didn't see her one time at the nursing home. She didn't ask me what I would need or how this would be possible. She was well aware of the trauma I had suffered from her husband and she disregarded it so that her tradition could be continued. My stepfather molested me. He tormented me for several decades and then I had my 'mini-stroke' in October of 2021 while staying with them after the loss of my job in Tennessee. I was struggling with exhaustion, slight weakness on my right side. I mean everything was off for a while. That Thanksgiving, my stepfather decided it would be a great time to confront me about living back in my childhood room. He screamed, he yelled, and he sought to degrade me. I was living in the very room under their roof where he had molested me. I had a job, I just couldn't find housing. It wasn't good enough, he still wanted to hurt me and in front of everyone. I was done with him in any family setting ever again. I fully intended that the next time I would see him, would be his funeral. Now, after my major stroke, I spent most of the time in my hospital bed, dealing with the resurfacing of repressed memories of the abuse, the trauma and the torment delivered by him. His horrendous caretaking of my mother who rarely addressed it to avoid her own abuse and torment. After all of this, my mother still assumed that I would use my limited energy to go to their home for a family meal? I had no bread to break with those people. A group of people I literally saw a handful of times during my recovery. My chosen family showed up a minimum of twice a month. I knew who wanted me around. The people that literally asked '*what do you need for us to bring you over?*' Not the people that said '*When are you coming?*' like everything was normal. It made me very angry initially, but I felt better when my mother made a snide, backhanded comment about my Thanksgiving plans. It honestly cheered me up how mad she was. Maybe, just maybe, she realized that I was done playing nice. You see, she also wanted those Hallmark movie moments. But she thought you get those moments with no work involved. '*Blood is thicker than water*' is utter bullshit! That is just a manipulation tactic for people who don't care to do the work for people they want as family in their lives. Society says that it is normal to deal with toxic people because they're blood family.

However, society also says that it is necessary to put the work into other relationships. Setting boundaries, respecting boundaries, actively listening and meeting them where they are, these are all things you would typically do for friends, why would you not do this for blood? I witnessed, my mother and stepfather laugh and joke with family but when they would leave and they were out of earshot, the most vicious and vile things would be said about the people they just hugged goodbye. I mean some of these people had photos on the walls of our home. The two faced behavior was always disgusting to me. I realized very young that this is not how you treat people you love. I learned the hardway when you're close to those people you aren't immune to that treatment it just gives them easier access to plunge the knife into your spine.

The Thanksgiving event was the starter event for what would eventually become a full family breakup. I'll talk about that later. Another factor for the separation came after a broken promise from my mother. My mother promised, after my apartment evicted me, that when I was able to be physically discharged and I had a steady income or disability, that she would help me get an apartment so that I would have a safe place to go. I put all of my faith into her promise, but I should have known better. This was the woman that co-signed for one brother's car and assisted with my other brother's house, but when I needed help with a co-signer while living under her roof, being asked to leave everyday, she just chose to complain about me asking her for help. Luckily, I found an apartment in 2021 and moved out, without a co-signer. I was proud of myself and the confidence was nice to get a yes through a hundred no's. I remember getting the phone call. I was picking up my best friend from her house because we were going to go to dinner. I was so excited to know that soon I would be leaving my childhood home, again. The very room where I experienced a betrayal unmatched by any other in my life. I remember going to check the place out. It was perfect for me, I didn't need much, just a place of my own. More room for my dog and a place free from abusers. I couldn't wait to have the opportunity to get out of my abuser's home and I felt the same about the nursing home, I just hoped it would happen before I lost everything. It didn't happen the way that I had hoped, but now I had to be out of the nursing home by December 3rd. Albeit with less money than before and a new eviction on my record. I knew it would be a challenge, but I was once told that I seem to always find a way to land on my feet.

November 26, 2023

Today is the Sunday after Thanksgiving and I'm still basking in the glow of a great holiday with friends and chosen family. Until this year my holidays were always more of a chore than a fun or magical time. I guess it was all that longing for families like those in the movies. The holidays always felt like a let down. Last year, during a rarely felt high point in my life, at least at that time, my thanksgiving was pretty confrontational with he who shall not be named. Those same feelings carried over to Christmas. So once again, my holidays were not something I could look back on with enjoyment. This year I spent time with people that exuded love and support. People that cared enough to learn my limitations and help. They were willing to rearrange their lives, to make accommodations for me, their chosen daughter. It truly was a great day. I have always felt like distancing yourself from things that make you unhappy is not a negative thing but this year has validated that theory in my life. It may hurt people or upset them that you're not fulfilling their expectations of you, but it's not about them. It's about your mental health and if they really care about you, they will understand. If they don't care, that is not your problem. I have learned in my 37 years on this earth that the person that cares most and will always care most about you in your life, is you! I chose to write today because life is coming at me quickly. I have to be out of the nursing home by December 3rd and I'm still waiting to hear back from the apartments that I've applied to. I'm waiting for my disability payment to come through so I can have some funds to get my life restarted. You'd think 11 months is long enough, but I can't control the process. Even with all of this anxiety, I'm still optimistic with my future. The old me would've been so uneasy, even devastated. But right now, I can see that my future is bright and there are new experiences coming my way.

It took a long time to get me to this point. The new me feels so content with what's coming that I'm willing to be patient. Rather than feeling like the universe is keeping me out in the cold. I feel like the universe has placed a warm blanket over my shoulders and has given me a reassuring hug. I am still astonished that what could be considered the worst time of my life so far now has turned into one of the best experiences. It's led to a whole new person. I see things so much differently now. I often wonder if I am pink clouding and after a huge breakthrough, that could be, since my brain chemistry is still recovering, but I plan to keep this feeling around. I feel like the direction my life is going will definitely keep me in that honeymoon phase. At least I hope it does. Only time will tell, but at least I can control how I react to things I can't control and I plan on maintaining my optimistic view to face those situations.

I am reminded that as I was writing my diary entries I was overwhelmed with excitement and fear. It was a crazy mix, like Redbull and vodka. An upper and a downer at the same time.

November 29, 2023

As you might be able to guess, my first book was approved for publishing! Sorry for the spoiler but you're reading the second book. LOL! I was so thrilled, my dreams at night have been filled with this book being published and the residual effects of it. I have foreseen so many things I hope come true, I'll be manifesting the 2024 that I want and deserve. I feel so accomplished just for being approved. But now we will see the fruits of my labor from trying to better myself. I can only hope that the first book does well enough to allow room for the second one to come out. I feel like my story is important, not just because it's mine. I'm biased, but I know I'm not the only person that has ever had to or will ever have to rebuild their life from zero. It doesn't matter the reason, it just matters that we rebuild in a healthy way. I know I'm not the only person to ever have those I'm on my way out of here in a few days and I am beyond excited! I can't wait to rejoin the real world again. It's not real here.

They make it so you have to be waited on. They keep your time for you. They monitor your food. They watch your every move, I was not able to rehabilitate fully in this environment. Whenever I get out of here I'll be able to practice daily, living without obstruction. I wasn't even able to practice walking on my own without being questioned or asked to sit back in my chair. Just because a place offers rehab, doesn't mean they are there for rehab. Rehab is so much more than just physical and occupational therapy.

After my first book was approved I really thought that my life would change. Much like my recovery, I still had work to do. That's ok though, I'm gonna get into this later too. Ironically, as I write this, my first book is experiencing a surge of energy and I have a newfound motivation to do so much more with my writing.

As my last days were spent in the nursing home waiting for my first disability payment, I started looking for people to help me move. To where? I wasn't entirely sure. I applied at a few apartments and was awaiting their responses. I had already received some rejections earlier in my stay at the nursing home. Little did I know, this would start another long line of rejection for me. It is absolutely insane what some of these apartments wanted for qualifications. I worked in housing for many years and I knew what kind of qualifications were needed. I was lucky enough to get a disability payment before I left the nursing home, I applied to like 10 places and I paid $50 - $100 per application. I knew that trying to get approved on my own first would be the best starting point. My mother would demand to know that I attempted to do it on my own first. By some grace of the universe, I was hoping at least one of them would work with me and I would be approved without any assistance. Within a few days I got a bunch of denials. I was rejected for having an eviction on my record, from the apartment I was just evicted from. I was rejected for a bad credit score, which plummeted from the credit cards that turned upside down from 11 months of no job, no income, no nothing. I was rejected for 'recent collections" from those same credit cards. I was rejected for my income, which I couldn't control, because of my disability. Even through all of the rejection, I still wasn't too down. I was looking forward to starting my new life. Even though I wasn't finding a permanent home situation, I found an extended stay hotel with fairly reasonable prices. I wasn't too excited to live in a hotel. Who would be excited to live in a hotel? I had to remind myself that living at a hotel I would at least have a bed, cable, internet, a fully accessible bathroom, a small but functional kitchenette, and my independence. More about it later. But back to me about to leave the nursing home.

December 2, 2023

I woke up to this being the last full day I will spend in a nursing home. Tomorrow, I get my room packed up and I leave for my temporary home for another. I found a hotel where you can stay for an extended time. I'll be staying there for at least 90 days and I'll spend that time relearning how to live alone again. I still have limitations that I need to work with until I get better. To say that I am feeling bittersweet right now, is accurate but also it doesn't speak to the volume of emotions I'm feeling. I never expected to be his sad to leave here. It's almost like walking the tightrope without the security net. At least here I knew I was safe-ish. Some of these people have been a part of my daily life for almost a year. Some were good relationships, some were not, but all made some sort of an impact on me. It's definitely emotional. When my social worker gave my discharge paperwork I almost cried. Partly because I was sad, partly because I was happy, mostly because I was anxious about how quickly real life was hurtling towards me. Also because a chapter of my life was closing and the new chapter starting and it is filled with unknowns. Signing my discharge papers made everything very real. I am not scared about this new chapter. I was welcoming it with open arms and optimism. I will not be waiting for the negative to hit me anymore. I don't need to manifest bad things on myself, especially in my current state. Today will be the last day of bingo, my last game of dominoes with my friends in this place. Wrtting this I realize how acclimated I became to the nursing home life. It's actually ironic to think about.

December 3, 2023

Today is the day! I woke up for the very last time in a nursing home. I was here for 293 days, over 41 weeks. That's 80.27% of my 2023. Roughly 7032 hours. It was such a large portion of my year, but in the big picture it really was a small portion of my life. 80.27% of my year but only about 2.19% of my life so far. When you think of it like that, it's definitely easier to swallow! My belongings were packed into about 5 large boxes and 10 small tote bags. That is my entire life. Everything I own was packed into so little. Before my stroke I lived in a two bedroom apartment. I fit everything I currently own into a handful of boxes and the amount of bags you could carry home from a grocery store trip. I wheeled out of the nursing home in my motorized chair and boarded their shuttle bus. The shuttle bus driver brought her sons to help move me and a friend from the bar I used to frequent offered her vehicle. I was sad, I really wanted to celebrate leaving, but that wasn't an option. I was still emotional from the goodbyes. The ride seemed to take forever but it was only 10 minutes. The whole way I kept thinking about my future. What would it all look like? What would the future hold for me? As I got closer to my new temporary home I felt a little anxiety come through. I wasn't moving to the most ideal situation. I didn't have a permanent place lined up yet so I had to pay for an extended stay hotel room. My chosen family offered me a space, but I had to learn how to live as independently as possible again. I didn't want to become dependent on others. It just wouldn't be a good way to heal and that is my focus at this point. I need to heal and recover as close to my original baseline as possible. That means constant relearning and constant activity. When I got to my extended stay hotel room, I loved it! This space is perfect. My bathroom is accessible to me. The space feels independent and this is how my rehabilitation should have been set up. It's basically a studio apartment but with a handicap accessible kitchen and bathroom. If I can figure it out, I'd like to open a true rehabilitation facility with rooms like this. I think I've set myself up for success in this place. I get to relearn in a place where I am comfortable and that is accessible for me. I feel like being here will send my ability to heal through the roof at warp speed!

This was the day I left the nursing home.

A NEW START

I got settled into the hotel after I was all moved in. None of my family offered to help. The moment I had been waiting for since January 13, 2023. I literally talked about my freedom, every single day and every single phone call. I reached out after I had gotten moved in and I asked if they could bring my clothes and hangers to me that they collected from my apartment before it was thrown away in my eviction. They went and packed my clothes, my purses and my dog, but when I asked them to bring my clothes and hangers to me so I could start my new life in a hotel room, they brought me 9 hangers and an old peacoat that I hadn't worn in years. They didn't bring my new peacoat with the beautiful leopard print lining, literally purchased weeks before my stroke. They brought me none of my dresses, none of the clothes I had before, and bitched the whole time while doing it. It was absolutely ludicrous. I learned to not ask for anything, because it just caused further contention. I took the hit on the chin and said fuck it. My family had proved to me many times, over the course of my nursing home stay, that I was a burden to them. I was a burden when I called, I was a burden when I wanted company, I was a burden when I didn't want my entire life thrown away, I was a burden when I simply wanted them to be a part of my patient care. I was a burden when they offered to take my dog in. I had to make up shit to have packages sent to my brother's house just to have him or my sister in law visit for just long enough to drop off my package. I was positive that they were annoyed with me, but I really wanted to see people. I would go weeks with no phone calls or visits, so I would manufacture a reason to have them come out.

They took in my dog, Appa, and promised to bring him to see me and they never did. Actually, I only got a few photos of him when I was recovering, and maybe one video and that was it. He was a rescue that I got while living in Tennessee. His owner, a resident at my property, was just going to take him to the pound. He was a giant 120 lbs bull mastiff lab mix. His owner was just going to throw him away. He was so sweet when he came for a meet and greet to see if I wanted him. I couldn't say no. He was fine at home initially, a little stand offish but later warmed up. His new surroundings were foreign to him and I learned the hard way that he had separation anxiety. When I came home from my first 8 hour shift away from him and he destroyed every blind, every pillow, knocked everything off of the kitchen counter and shit twice in the house, I figured he needed some extra love. It took a while to earn his trust, but we eventually had a great relationship. He would sleep in my bed, he would go on trips with me, he was my child. I finally learned what it was like to love another living thing. I didn't want children, but I had my guy. He caused me so much drama, but I loved him nonetheless. He is the reason I cried so many times during my recovery. I missed him so much and my family lied to me. They had him at their home, 10 minutes away from the nursing home and still just couldn't find the time to bring him to see me. I felt betrayed.

My first night in the hotel was nothing crazy. Actually, it was kind of nice. I didn't have shitty CNA's bothering me. Or horny old Tommy trying to make out with me or peering around the corner to catch a glimpse of me changing. I ordered some food and tried to learn about my new surroundings. I explored the hotel and its grounds. I went to bed late and woke up in the afternoon the next day. What does one do when living on disability? I didn't know either, but I felt that I deserved a late start to the day. I was finally free. Later, I felt like if I was going to be back in the real world, I should be a part of it. I knew that I could write, so I told myself to start writing. The publishing company I used for my first book, was a very expensive lesson in how to self publish and market, but I assumed it was the way to do it. I was always waiting for updates from the publisher on the edit, or the cover photo, or the other aspects of the book, but I learned different lessons along the way.

I spent that first week learning about my new surroundings. I was good and everyday I worked through new challenges and continued my recovery. I got to December 13th and I was officially 11 months after the most devastating day of my life. I woke up naturally, fully rested but realized that I missed my ride to my doctor's appointment. I went from extremely upset and disappointed to remembering that we were working differently now. I took a few deep breaths and thought about how to handle the situation. I knew I couldn't go back in time. So I started by rescheduling my appointments and then started doing some cleaning. What had started off as a rollercoaster of emotions, wasn't over yet. I was cleaning up my little kitchenette area and when I bent down to pick up something that fell, I too fell. This was my biggest fear of living on my own, I even asked my physical therapists to help me in this exact scenario. They didn't help me with it at all. In fact one of them told me to never not have my phone on my person because if I fell, I would need to call 9-1-1. They knew that is what I wanted, but they didn't care. Further affirming that the people in that nursing facility do not actively listen. I appreciate the good advice, but they didn't know that I was a fighter. This would be a fight!

My balance had been improving everyday since my stroke, but for some reason this was the day that my balance gave out and I fell to the ground. It was rough and I was very nervous. With my weakened left side, I couldn't get up and down like everyone else. Unsure of what to do in this situation, I laid there on the floor and cried for a few moments. I had myself a pity party and then I decided to call the ambulance. I was able to grab my phone off of the counter next to where I fell and I started to dial 9-1-1. As I went to hit send to start the call I paused. I asked myself 'do you really need to call an ambulance to get up?' I put my phone down, wiped my tears and formulated a plan. After scanning the room I came up with a few options. I thought about using the rails in the handicap bathroom, but I had concerns. I was aware of certain limitations and I wasn't so sure it would work. I decided to move on to plan B. Luckily, my room was a "suite" so I had a little couch in my room that was also a sleeper. It was heavy duty and I could use it in a number of ways to try to get up. I needed to get to the bed area. I began scooting myself across the room while steering my wheelchair from the floor in between scoots.

I finally got to the area where my bed and couch were. I took a moment to rest and regain the strength I used to scoot myself across the room. Before I got started I began telling myself that I was not going to be a victim of this stroke. I was much stronger than the time that CNA found me and rolled her eyes at me like my first fall in the nursing home. I was going to find the strength to get off of this floor. I attempted a few things with my bed because the frame was also heavy duty. I discovered that my left knee, my stroke affected knee, was not able to handle weight long enough to get my other foot under me to push up and at least get on the bed.

I reassessed and searched for plan C. I noticed that the couch was pretty low to the ground. I am a tall person and I knew that I could probably push myself onto the couch and I was able to get most of the way, but needed a little boost. I stopped pushing and went back to sitting on the ground. I moved my chair to be between me and the bed. I started pushing on the floor to get my back on the couch cushion again. Once I was on my back I had to get my butt on the couch. That is when I used my chair to push off and finally crossed the threshold.

When I got my upper half and my butt on the couch, I had to rest again. I was breathing heavily and I was pretty tired, but a feeling of accomplishment began washing over me. I laid on the couch long enough to get my breathing under control and I adjusted my position to sit up on the couch without sliding off the couch.

A few days after my stroke, the hospital started my recovery process and wanted to get me out of my bed and propped me up in a chair in my room. My best friend was sitting with me and we were chatting like old times and that's when I had to pee. I had a blanket on me and I had my urinal with me. I positioned the urinal to pee, but I felt uncomfortable, so I moved forward to position myself more comfortably. That is when my "dead weight" pulled me down to the floor. My friend was scared and I was embarrassed, but after the spill, a doctor came in and spoke to me. They told me that it is easier to stay planted in a seat when you lean forward, because your butt is pointed in the direction of the back of the seat. If you lean back, your butt has a potential of positioning to the front of the chair. This makes sense, but I was nervous that my upper body leaning forward was dangerous too.

Ironically this is a lesson that always stuck with me and I needed it now. I pointed my butt towards the back of the couch and got seated correctly. As I got seated properly. I hadn't gotten up from a seat this low, but I started rocking to get some momentum As I pushed up on the first attempt and didn't have the leverage. By my 3rd attempt, I was on my feet. I had my chair close by, so I had stability and I was able to take a few steps to get to my chair. I finally got in my chair and I started to cry again. I was on the floor crying an hour before. I struggled, I fought, I scooted and I formulated. I was finally able to get off of the floor. The feeling of accomplishment flooded through me. In my pre-stroke life I could just stand up from the ground. It was so easy. I could do it sober. I could do it piss pants drunk. I remember vividly, it would take me less than a few seconds. Now it took me about an hour. I felt so accomplished and I went back to cleaning my kitchenette area. I continued my day and finished cleaning up. When I was done I sat in my chair and was exhausted. All of my energy was used up from struggling to get off of the floor and then cleaning my kitchen area. As I sat there watching my iPad I was overcome with exhaustion. I transferred myself to my bed and took a long well deserved nap.

The next few weeks were much easier and I had avoided any big drama, but behind all of that non-drama loomed Christmas. Christmas was another holiday that was always associated with negative memories. My stepfather always used Christmas as a time for him to take center stage. He always wanted confirmations that his presents were good, even though he always bought my mom watches, or jewelry that she never wore, or he would buy her clothes that wouldn't fit. My mom's Christmas' were often filled with her being disappointed, even if she tried to hide it. My empathy always got the best of me. If he wasn't disappointing people with his shitty gifts, he would be screaming and slamming doors or making everyone focus on him. This was throughout my entire life. Whenever someone or something else was on center stage, that meant that he wasn't being paid attention to. Like a toddler that no one was paying attention to, he had to misbehave or through a fit. As Christmas continued to creep closer I was contemplating a very impactful decision. During my time in the nursing home I had a friend talk to me about boundaries. I realized after our talk that people had been setting up boundaries on me but I was not setting boundaries on others. 'Blood is thicker than water' was what I was raised on. I was not familiar with setting boundaries for my family. That was over. I had spent the last end of my recovery actively setting boundaries and ending relationships with people that were not listening to my boundaries. I reserved my time for people willing to earn the relationship. Part of my recovery was spent with resurfacing memories of the vile negativity of my step-father. I decided I had no reason to have any relationship with him moving forward. I had been sacrificing my mental health by keeping him as a part of my life for the sake of my 'family'. The 'family' that saw me a handful of times collectively throughout my stroke recovery. The 'family' that told me that I was stressing them out. The 'family' that proved to me that they were all about lip service and appearances. I spoke earlier about the phrase 'blood is thicker than water'. I've said that this phrase is absolutely a manipulation tactic meant to obligate you to people without anyone having to put the work in. My 'family', my blood had proven to me that they didn't care about the emotional work it actually takes to build a bond with someone. I was tired of having a relationship with people that continued to let me down, over and over again. So after much thought and weighing the "consequences", I made a very important decision.

After moving into the hotel room, an apartment community was just being finished across the street. I applied there. They were all ground level, so no stairs. They were one bedroom, so all the room I needed. They were just remodeled. They were perfect for me. When I applied I spoke with the manager to discuss my situation. She understood and when I got my denial, she went to bat for me with her regional management. Unfortunately, it didn't matter. The management company upheld the denial because of my credit score. They wanted a credit score that could qualify me for my own home, btw. So I pulled the nuclear option and asked my mom to help co-sign. This was another 'family' thing I have dealt with my whole life. My mom always focused on her credit score and it always gave '*my precious*' energy. I got the denial and I reached out to my mom and explained that I had gotten a denial on a great apartment, right across the street, newly renovated, ground level, and for only $825 per month. The hotel had a rate of $1200 per month my first 90 days. Since she did tell my social worker that she would co-sign an apartment for me if I had an income, it was within budget and I could pay without issue. I was able to meet that criteria. You would think a person whose first born child just had her whole life uprooted and flipped on its head, would want to help because "blood is thicker than water" right? Also, she did offer. Past promises didn't matter in this case. In my mother's true nature and in a situation I knew well, I asked my mother to help me get into a permanent home with a much more manageable payment and in our usual game of 'Mother giveth, Mother taketh away'. My mother who gaveth me hope that I may be able to rebuild my life after losing literally everything, tooketh away all of that hope after saying that she would help. Suddenly, the initial qualifications weren't enough. Now she wasn't willing to co-sign. Apparently I was rebuilding entirely from the start with zero help. Part of me believed that it was because she focused on her illness and recovery. So, I tried giving grace. The other part of me truly believed it was because she wanted to see me fail. So, that grace faded quickly. if I failed, I was still the fuck up. I've always felt a distance with my mother. Was it because her mother showed me the love she didn't receive? Was it because I made her "happy" marriage more difficult? Was it because I was part of the LGBTQ? Was it because my stroke might be overshadowing her cancer? I don't know the answer. What I do know is I tried my best my entire life to prove I was worthy of this woman's love and still I never felt like it was reciprocated. This was another moment where I was let down. I know it sounds so privileged to complain that my mommy wouldn't co-sign an apartment for me. As I mentioned earlier, she literally co-signed my brother's car and paid for part of the down payment for my other brother's house. Because my role was supposed to be the family fuck up, I'm sure that's how they will tell it, I was not worthy of the help. It was at this point that I didn't see much point in holding back anymore. I had had enough of sparing people's feelings. I made the decision to write a personal letter to my mom. In this letter I explained my absence in her life because of her husband. I explained how my relationship was strained with my brothers and I explained how I didn't like how my mother was treated by her husband/caregiver. This was a letter to help her understand where I was and she had the opportunity to meet me where I was. Here are some excerpts from that letter.

Letter to Mom

Mom,

I felt bad the other day when we got off the phone, I felt like I could hear the pain in your voice. I don't have a lot that I could get you for Christmas, You can fulfill most of your own needs. So I figured I would write you this letter to help you understand where I'm at. This is not to attack you, or meant to make you feel bad in any way, so please know this is written with good intent and to give you clarity about me and the person I have become because of all of my recent experiences. I wanted to write the letter because I tend to get emotional very quickly and this way what I want to say will be better communicated. This letter doesn't require a reply. First, let me start out with I love you very much! I know in your life you've been through the wringer. And I don't want my current choices to be another trauma you feel you have to survive. I know that you know what it feels like to have your body betray you. What you may not understand is the feeling of abandonment by everyone you love. When I had this stroke, It was the most terrifying thing I've ever experienced. When I was confined to my hospital bed, I had hours and hours a day to do nothing but think and ponder and live inside my own head. All I wanted was someone to talk to. I began placing high value on those that were reaching out to me.

I felt I started the letter off with truth and with vulnerability. I was filling her in on actual changes in my life. She hadn't seen me in person for months. We have had conversations, but nothing in depth. I was trying to reach out and help her understand me. I moved forward to tell her that I was spending time with people that saw me as a valuable member of their family unit. I also explained that one of my brothers was already separating himself from everyone, so I wasn't expecting him to be present anyway.

As far as my relationship with your husband, my dislike for him is not new. Knowing now as an adult what the ideal stepparent should be, he was no father to me, he wasn't a stepfather. I didn't have a father growing up. After the fiasco last thanksgiving, I honestly didn't feel like I ever needed to see him again. And really I felt that way after the family visited me in Pennsylvania. I write a lot about the face value of relationships and when someone treats you one way and then says things to make you feel better about everything, it is manipulative and fake. I spent a lot of time between my childhood and adulthood trying to keep up appearances with him, for the family's sake because if I didn't I felt like I was the problem. After realizing that I can't allow myself to bottle up my feelings and keep them repressed anymore, I do not plan on keeping up the facade anymore. From now on people will get the energy from me that they give. I also will not engage with people that I don't want to engage with. He is not someone I plan to engage with. I find him toxic and a terrible influence for my niece and nephew in their early years of development. But I am not their parent, so unfortunately for them they are exposed to him. Not even to get into the way he fucked with my head as a kid and the way he treats you. Maybe it's not entirely his fault. Maybe sometimes his brain has trouble differentiating between a husband and a caretaker, but he chose to be both but isn't acting like either. When you are able to say things to me like "I know what it's like to fight for my freedom, because I do it everyday!" I don't like the way he treats the people I love. Most of you will let him get away with the way he acts and brush it off as, "that's just him." I have no obligation to continue playing pretend with him. And to speak on another point, you made a comment about how he has been doing stuff for me and isn't even allowed to see me. I never asked for his help, he has interjected himself. I don't plan on feeling bad for taking advantage of him in my time of need; changing a battery doesn't make up for years and years of torment. I'm sorry. I wrote in my book about how I always want-

ed a family like the famous ones on TV so I empathize with your expectations of a family but those families only exist on TV or in movies.

I moved on to talk about how those families are nice for a story, but that they are not real. I also spoke about a time when my very first physical therapist told me that it would be a good idea to have a family member come and see how my recovery is going. I reached out to my closest brother who lived minutes away from the hospital that I was recovering in. He made an excuse and declined to be a part of my recovery. When I mentioned this to my chosen family they immediately volunteered. I explained the impact it had on me to have someone cheering me on. This is what friends or family should be. They should be your cheering section. They should be there to lift you up and you should be there to lift them up. This is what a cheering section does. Do you think they loved cheering me on when I told them that I put a sock on for the first time? Probably not, but they still cheered! My chosen family took a video of me walking and sent it to other friends. It felt great, but also incredibly unusual that my blood was not there taking videos, it was my chosen family. That meant a lot to me. I finished my letter advising that I was a new woman and I was changing in many ways. I explained that my recovery was going to require me to set boundaries. There is no point in setting boundaries, without following through with them. I put love, care and truth into this letter with the hope that I would be taken seriously. My mom had a chance to receive this information and simply meet me where I was. Did she meet me where I was? No, she actually went as far as to take a personal letter between my mother and myself and shared it with my brothers. This wasn't surprising to me. My mom was a person that loved to share other people's personal business because it took attention off of her. Of course, this is something that was used as a weapon. If she wanted the attention on her, she would keep other people's business a secret. When she wanted the attention off of her, no secret was safe. Kind of like the letter I shared with my Mother. It was an explanation of my mental health and distance and it later shared with my brothers. She continued to take my phone calls and answer texts like nothing was a problem. I'm assuming because she knew I wouldn't be happy.

December 30, 2023

There hasn't been as much drama to write about lately; life has been truly fabulous and new in so many ways. I did spend the holidays with people that I chose, and not people I had to pretend to like. I told my mom, I would no longer be spending time with her, if her husband is around. And since he doesn't like to be out of the loop, I guess I may not see my mom a lot in the future. This did make me feel bad ,but there were options on her side for her to see me without putting me in the path of my abuser. Whether she isn't recognizing those options by accident or is choosing to not see them, that is on her. I'm sure I sound heartless, but I am protecting myself moving forward. No one in my life will care about my well being like I care about my well being. I was explaining the situation to a friend, and I told him that I was choosing to fight the war for my peace. Unfortunat-

ely, this is true and never a fun thing; this is me setting those boundaries that we've been talking about. Boundaries are required for me to continue my recovery. For me to recover correctly, I need to be in the right mindset. To do that, I need to set boundaries to avoid situations that are likely to change my mental health for the worse. I believe recovery is a lot like a snowflake. They are all the same, as in they are all frozen water, but they are all different. All recovery is recovery, but everyone's recovery looks different. What we're recovering from is different and the way to the finish line is different for each one of us. We look for the path that gets us there and we prepare for a battle. Sometimes that battle throws us off our path, but as long as we find our way back to our path, recovery is still possible.

This was a very difficult time for me, but I actually felt a lot of relief. I didn't have the weight of these expectations on me anymore. The wieght of obligation, The wieght of family. The wieght of tradition. No longer burdening my mental health. I chose me. A decision that was overdue.

December 31, 2023

Today is the last day of 2023. It's definitely bittersweet. Fourteen days from now will be the one year anniversary of my stroke. As I wrote this today, I imagined what the old me would have thought about this whole stroke experience. The old me saw this as a tragedy and just knew that my life was over. The new me remembers the experience but also the lessons learned from it. While 2023 may look like a shit year for most, the truth is, so many things in me started to heal and i'm grateful for 2023. Here is to a better year in 2024, but more importantly, here is to growth and healing.

NEW YEAR, NEW ME?

A few days into the new year, I was having a great day. I had a good conversation with my mom and even felt like I was heard. It felt like I was heading towards something new. For a little while, I believed that my letter had done what I was hoping it would do. Later that day, I was doing some schoolwork. I started working on my Bachelors in 2019 after realizing that I needed a college degree to qualify for a regional manager role in the housing industry. In my opinion, my experience and successful history should have spoken much louder than a college degree, but they didn't see it that way. I worked on my bachelors in business through the University of Phoenix online and I did that through job site changes, through COVID-19 and I was in my last year with only seven courses left at the time of my stroke. When I got to the hotel, I decided to complete my degree. The way I looked at it, my restart could be jumpstarted by a degree. I felt recovered enough to try to finish it, so I re-enrolled and gave myself a new purpose. I took a break away from my schoolwork that day and I jumped on my Facebook to doom scroll a little. I saw a friend was getting rid of a play kitchen and immediately thought of my niece and nephew. I sent them a message asking for details. I also messaged my brother to see if he would like it for the kid's playroom. I thought my brother would not want more room taken up in his house and that is when I remembered how much fun I had growing up with my aunts, uncles and cousins. I thought that I would make some space in my little hotel room and I would take the play kitchen so that when my niece and nephew would come over they would have something to play with. The first time they came over, they made a fort under the bed. It was funny, but if I wanted to be able to visit with my brother, sister-in-law, niece and nephew, the kids should have something to entertain them at least for a minute. I planned to surprise them. I messaged my friend and asked if she was willing to bring the play kitchen to me. She agreed. I moved the furniture in the room and prepared a space designated for playing. Right as I finished moving furniture, I mean the second that I took one last look to see if it worked and was functional for me, my phone dinged. I got a text from my brother. '*We don't need it.*' I then got another message '*I also think what you wrote was very messy so we're not totally happy with you right now.*' Great! I was immediately flushed with sadness, when my brother was not happy with me, I was not able to see him or the kids. I learned this in the nursing home. Whenever I was 'stressing him out' or I was a burden, I was inevitably going to be far more lonely for a while. I wrote that letter to set boundaries with my mother. I wanted to express to HER why I refused to spend time with her, if my stepfather was around and now this personal letter that I sent her was going to be used as a weapon against me. I didn't care why he was "not happy". Once again I felt betrayed. Once again, something I was trying to do to make our experiences better when we did see each other was now used to make me the villian. I don't know if it was the light that I shined on my stepfather being a danger to be around my niece and nephew. I don't know if he was upset because I shined a light on his emotional abuse towards the entire family. All I did know was that I stood by what I said and I was over being gaslit to believe I was the one in the wrong or that I was over thinking his actions. I was over it. I just went through a major medical event and I was in the process of rebuilding my entire life. I was over the manipulation. After a cool down period and some small conversation asking my mom why she shared that letter when it was personal, I gave up. I was used as a family punching bag. I was mocked. I was made fun of and at the end of the day, I was receiving nothing in return. 37 years of living with these people proved to me that I was still an outsider to all of them. By the end of the day everyone was blocked, everyone was cut off. My phone number was changed and I have since moved from the hotel. More on that later.

Everyday, I miss my family. Everyday, I remember those moments when they made me laugh. Everyday, I remember riding together in the car, even on small trips.

Like the time we were going for gas and we all watched my brother try to use a speedway membership card at the shell gas station. He was so comically frustrated. We all nearly died laughing. Everyday, I remember my niece and nephew and our good times together. I am then reminded of being told I am stressing people out simply because I wanted to see them. I remember being incredibly vulnerable recovering from what we now know was a small stroke and being asked repeatedly '*When are you moving out?*' I remember being scolded for not going on a family vacation to Destin, FL because I was clearly an afterthought. Not to mention 19 hours in a car with an emotionally unregulated man child.

It is hard to walk away from people you have known your whole life, but you learn to continue on. You learn to live a life free of other people's expectations of you. You learn to live life by your standards and by your expectations. This is not something many people get to experience, but when we do get the chance that is when we experience the world of endless opportunities. Societal standards tend to be referred to as 'normal', but normal doesn't really exist and it certainly doesn't fit everybody. I didn't want 'normal'. I wanted the life that I dreamed of my whole life. I wanted freedom. I once had a vivid dream of me living in a city setting, I was in front of a computer and I knew in my dream that I was a successful novelist. I felt my freedom and I was extremely fem presenting, this was long before I came out as trans, btw. I was living my life, unbothered by society and their judgement. This is a hot topic right now with Donald causing all of the division in this country. People are learning the lesson I discussed earlier. People are learning that *'blood is thicker than water'* is a manipulation tactic to just continue harmful 'traditions'. Even if 'tradition' is something like participating in events with uncle Benny, Uncle Benny is the creepy uncle that they tell all of the kids to stay away from, but they still put kids around Uncle Benny. These are the people that want to conserve *'tradition'*. They are willing to subject their children to creepy uncle Benny. Why stay connected to a person that you would not let watch your children alone? Because *'blood is thicker than water'?* They have been manipulated to believe that even though a weird creepy uncle could possibly harm children, it's ok to subject their little ones to him. NO! Stop conserving traditions that perpetuate harm. Trump has not divided Democrats and Republicans. He has divided traditions and morals. It's kind of funny how the party they try to demonize and label as woke baby killers actually have more advanced morals than them. It's funny how the '*satan worshipers*' actually exhibit more Christian-like values than the christians that cheer on a system that creates hungry children, homeless people and attacks on immigrants. That day was rough, but it had been a long time coming. I had been holding back from doing that for a while. The betrayal of the letter was huge, but that also meant that I was the one being subjected to behind-the-back gossiping. The rest of that week was different for me.

January 13, 2024

Today is the anniversary of my stroke and I have spent the day enjoying my new independence. I thought many times about where I was by the end of the day on January 13th, 2023 compared to where I am today, Janu-

ary 13, 2024. Last year I was in a hospital bed, thinking about how I would sleep in a foreign bed, in a foreign place, filled with unanswered questions and unknown circumstances. I was worried about my dog and I was in tears. I was terrified for our future! Tonight, I will lay my head on a pillow, granted, it isn't mine, but it's familiar and I'll be sleeping in a place where I am comfortable. I, ironically, will still be worried about my dog, but that's because he is my baby and I'll always be worried about him, but I'm not in tears. I know where he is and I know he's got people that love him around him. A year ago, I could have not woken up at all and I probably would have been ok with it. I'm now looking forward to waking up tomorrow. Everyday behind me is a day closer to the destiny I have been manifesting for years. It's also another day of recovery that I was able to get through successfully. Today could have been a day filled with bad memories and replaying vivid nightmares and traumas. Instead, I chose to make today about comparing then to now so that I could reflect on my accomplishments. It is very important to any recovery to have those days that you reflect on your progress. We may not be invincible, but we are capable of bouncing back. I mean look at Jeremy Renner, he was run over by a giant piece of machinery and he probably could have given up from the pain of the broken bones alone. But he didn't give up. He kept trying! Whether your recovery is physical or mental. Whether you're recovering from substance abuse or health issues, every kind of recovery requires one thing. It is the easiest and the most difficult thing to do and that is to keep trying! There will be obstacles along the path of recovery and they can cause you to detour from your path. As long as you keep trying, you'll get back on track. I almost said you'll see the finish line, but recovery sometimes has no finish line. We can have goals we're achieving, but that doesn't mean we stop trying. It means we've reached a milestone, I think once you've reached a milestone don't slow down, speed up. Keep setting goals, keep reaching them and continue to prove your efforts to yourself. I created a vision board for the first time in my life because I feel like resolutions are out dated, just like chain restaurants and video rental. A vision board is just a set of goals, you look at daily and can't forget or ignore. I created this board so I can constantly check in with my-

self about where I envisioned myself in 2024. I recommend everyone has a vision board. It keeps you honest with yourself.

In full disclosure my original visionboard didn't stand the test of time. The great thing about my writing is that I sometimes inspire myself. I'm that good! Lol! But I am biased. So I suppose that I will work on an updated vision board. I had some things on my vision board that just didn't happen and it was discouraging, but I continued on. I decided to focus on stuff to keep my head above water. I put my hopes and dreams on the back burner. In fact it was around this time that I started really struggling with my ability to find housing. I also found that this time I went from saying *"I'm okay"* to actually saying *"I'm happy!'* The first time someone asked how are you? When I replied *"I'm happy!"* I started to cry. It looked contradictory but I was so happy to be able to say I was happy and mean it, It was true, not embellishment. I was not only happy, but I was happy while living in a hotel room, on the lowest income I've ever had, with the least amount of personal possessions. I still found a way to be happy. I found happiness in my daily life, I found happiness in showering without a CNA in the room. I found happiness in making my own meals. I found happiness in so many things that people take for granted everyday with their typical physical abilities. I learned that you shouldn't take the little things for granted. We are all one medical event from wishing we could wipe our own asses, or shower without help.

A few weeks into 2024 a friend messaged me to chat and told me that she had broken up with her boyfriend and her grandma's health was declining. She said that 2024 had already been shit. We had just gotten into the new year. I was filled with new found happiness and optimism. I sent a message reminding her to focus on what we can control. Why do we take on the drama or the trauma about things that we can't control? I promise you, you have enough bad circumstances coming your way. You don't need to take on other situations as yours to have something to complain about in your life. I reminded her that she cannot control how a guy feels about her. She can only control the way she processes the loss and then she can control moving on. Same with her grandma. She couldn't control the health of an old woman. She could only control how it affects her and she could prepare herself for the future and whether or not it will include grandma.

I think my positivity became toxic to some people because I wasn't having bad days. My friend kind of let the conversation die and I once again felt like my trying to help wasn't what she wanted. I didn't feel like feeding into the idea that your year is already bad. There was so much year to go and that's all I wanted her to focus on.

Prior to my stroke I got very involved with men. I was just finding my footing as an adult woman and I decided to take advantage of the attention I was being given. I started randomly hooking up and going home with people. I found myself putting myself in some very dangerous situations. I have some stories about situations I put myself in that porn directors would love to replicate! Now that I was living on my own, that was now an option again. Unfortunately, it was an option in the nursing home too, I never felt the urge, or felt sexy enough to ever have any kind of sex in the nursing home,

But yes, men reached out to me to come to the nursing home, just to have sex! Love is something that I have always wanted in my life, but always lacked. So, I made 'Love' part of my vision board. I assumed I wasn't worthy. I told myself that I wasn't meant to have love in my life. I was going to try anyway. I am worthy of love. I am worthy of a real partner in my life. In pursuit of fulfilling my vision board I put my heart back out on the line. Unfortunately, my best option was to start online dating.

During my stay in the nursing home, I started talking to someone. He seemed accepting and genuine. I was expecting nothing great, but I figured this could be something. We never know until we know, do we? As our conversations continued in my time at the hotel, we finally decided to meet up. He drove about 2 hours to come to see me. When we met up, we did our greetings then we decided to chat for a bit. We chatted for a while and then he asked if he could kiss me. We made out for a while and he even got to feel me up. The heat died down and he ended up leaving, not without talking about how he is disappointed that we didn't do more. I just wasn't ready to jump back into sex like that. When he left he didn't text me again until the next day. When he did finally text me he told me that he had unbearable driving anxiety and didn't want to make that drive again. I wasn't buying it. I will say I do like to believe people, but It just seemed too weird that he managed to get here once and then was suddenly not able to do it again. I would think the more you make a trip like that, the easier it gets. Either way, I'm not stupid, he made it clear that he was not happy that he didn't get his dick wet. He did all the things they do. He even found a reason to flash his crotch at me, to "show me tattoos". He 'adjusted' himself while telling me I was hot. He used the bathroom with the door open. All to no avail. I was not ready. There was more to me than a sex object for men to use. I was a little upset that he pulled away because he was actually nice to talk to. I thought there was an emotional connection. But it seems in this world today, men don't really know how to connect emotionally. Their emotional connection seems to be with their penis. This might be why I never aligned with being a 'man'. Males who align with being a man are cisgender. Females who align with the gender of woman are cisgender. I didn't align with being a boy or with being a man. That's what being transgender is. Anyway, I knew that my hopes for a relationship with him were not likely. So, I hit the dating apps again. I met a guy that lived minutes from the hotel that I was living at. We spoke for a few days and then he wanted to meet me in person. He offered to bring me lunch and we could meet and learn about each other. At least that's what he said. It sounded nice and he said he understood my limitations. I'd reminded him multiple times. We set the time and the date. I was very excited. I felt like I had a good bullshit detector, but I got got. When he arrived, I went to the lobby to meet him. I brought him to my little apartment, or hotel room, but it was my starter apartment. He was holding a bag with our lunch in it. Once in the room, he pulled out a sandwich, a bottle of water and a Kit Kat bar from the gas station. I realized at that moment that this would be the first and last time I would be dealing with him.

He immediately sat very close to me. This is when I was glad my wheelchair was just for one. Part of me wanted to just ask him to leave. Part of me wanted to see that I was just heavily guarded and I was overthinking it all. A small part of me was enjoying the company and the attention. His next move was to massage my shoulders. I had never had a shoulder massage. I really enjoyed it. Especially after my stroke. The muscle tension could be unbearable at times. I guess I enjoyed it too much. I let my guard down and then he offered to do my back. I needed to be out of my chair and in a more comfortable position. I transferred from my chair to my bed, where I laid on my stomach and awaited more of this massage he offered. He started in on my shoulders and then suddenly he stepped up near my head, dick out! Waiving it at me. I was put off. Anyone would be. I had a moment where I thought about screaming, or fighting. The dangerous part of me reminded me, you have to start somewhere, so maybe it wasn't so bad to give in a little bit to temptation. I leaned my head forward and put him in my mouth. A few back and forth motions into the act he put his hand on the back of my head and pushed me into him. I was not prepared to be forced into anything. So I bit down lightly into his penis. He immediately let go of my head and pulled away from me. I sat up and played it off like a reaction from my muscle spasms from my stroke. Those were real, by the way. He took my fake apology as a queue to finish himself off in his hand. I'm not sure how that was the message given but that's what he did and I just let him. I was not willing to jeopardize my safety any further. He finished and as he washed his hand, he got a "phone call" from his brother who needed him right away. He quickly left and was never heard from again. Legend has it that he tells stories now of nearly having his dick bitten off by a disabled trans woman. That's a joke but I imagine there is some truth to it. All I can confirm is that when I had the time to look back and realize how my fast and dangerous path was heading for self destruction and was only detoured by my stroke. I came to the realization that I was not placing value on myself and I was letting men just have me. I'm not sure about everyone, but every man that I ever had any sex with has taken a piece of me with him. A piece of my heart or a piece of my empathy or just a random piece of me. I look at myself and sometimes feel like swiss cheese because of all of the pieces of me that men have taken when they leave. I'm a hopeless romantic and I think that is why men always take a piece of me with them. Even when I used men back how they used me, they still came out a winner, because they got a piece of me that I will never get back. The worst part is that they don't even know what they've taken. If they do know, they don't care. They just come back and want more, even if I'm in a nursing home. That wasn't enough to stop them.

I assumed that somewhere down that path someone would like what I offered so much that they would scoop me up and want something exclusive. That never happened. It didn't matter how long we spoke or if we took it slow. They all found their opening and got what they were after and then disappeared. I mentioned in my first book that this was a common occurrence. I figured my wheelchair might scare them away. Unfortunately not enough. I should have known it didn't matter, I literally had guys that wanted to come to the nursing home to have sex with me. They were willing to come to a medical setting with people screaming in pain and the chaos of room alarms going off just to have sex. It truly is ludicrous to me how these guys are so hard up, they will lie to a disabled, transwoman in a nursing home just to fulfill a fetish of theirs. As I write this transgender people are being attacked all over the country. Laws are being passed. Licenses are being revoked. It is disgusting to me that when people don't fit into a mediocre binary box, people want to legislate you away. The worst part is that they fear us enough to want to legislate against us, but they also fetishize us enough to want to fuck us. It's so sick and those people that do this are ignored when they are caught on trans porn sites or with trans sex workers. They continue to focus on the trans people, not the pervs. While they rape women and children and then lie and point the finger at bathrooms. I honestly can't tell if people are upset about us living our true and authentic selves or if they are offended that we deny their standards. I think the first option is more likely and they just can't stand the fact that we are able to disconnect from their societal standards and still be happy. Our entire lives, we are expected to live by what society says. We are told *"blood is thicker than water"*, Men don't cry, Women aren't loud. The moment they encounter someone that is still living a great life against those rules, they lose their fucking minds.

It's unfortunate that we are met with immediate anger and vitriol. If we were met with just genuine curiosity and people wanting to know more, we could all learn together. They don't actually care that trans people exist or that we are verified by science and nature. They want something to be mad about. Or something new to put their dicks in. It is just absurd. This is something that Trump has exacerbated with our country. People that need the focus taken off of themselves now have a place to direct attention. People that need some drama in their life now have manufactured drama in their lives. Trump needed as many distractions as possible to avoid accountability. The regressive right needed a start to peel away at the rights of the 2SLGBTQIA+. (If you bitch about initialisms, we will just add more letters, numbers and/or symbols. Don't fuck with us, we are petty. We have an advanced placement class in petty, we take it right after how to tuck or bind.)

Anyway, back to the main story, I just bit a man's dick and he left the hotel. A few days later, tragedy struck. Well that's dramatic, but it was a little bit of a tragedy to me. I had been going to physical therapy on my own, more growth on my part as I was keeping my schedule independently , I was scheduling my own transportation, timing my rides, my appointments and holding to them. These were all things that were done for me when I was in recovery. I had gotten on the bus, in my wheelchair, to go to therapy. My chair was working fine. They got me to therapy, they unhooked my chair and when I went to wheel off the bus and my chair suddenly was acting really weird. When I would push the joystick forward to go forward my chair would turn right and then pull left. When I pulled back to reverse, it would try going forward while also turning to the left. The wiring was shorting out and I even started smelling hot wires. The driver went into the therapist office and a few therapists came out to help me off the bus, my chair was not working. I used mobility equipment at the therapy office to get around. I did my full therapy session. When I was done, they wheeled me onto the bus and I transferred to a bus seat. When I finally got home I had to have the hotel staff bring me my rollator from my room. So that I could walk back into the hotel and get to my room. Luckily, I had used my personality to establish a relationship with these people and they were kind enough to help me in ways that I was not sure I would have had available while living independently. They helped with a package here and there. They were amazing to me and the best that I could have asked for with my first independent living situation after my stroke. My walk to my room was fine and I felt accomplished. This started a few weeks of having no wheelchair in my daily life. I knew it wouldn't be easy.

February 6, 2024

It's been 15 days since my wheelchair went haywire and I've been on my walker full time. Things have been tiring but really smooth. I did have one falling incident, but I'm not hurt and there was no permanent damage. The process of getting up was similar to last time both in length and procedure. I can feel myself taking much better steps when I walk, I can feel myself getting stronger. My left arm has even become more cooperative. Before when I would walk, my left arm would stay curled up and tight to my body, but I've been able to extend my arm straight to my side lately. I even had a missed step and it seemed like I might fall again, but my arm reached for the wall helping me to balance out again. I am no longer as nervous as I was when my chair died. I've been able to get around pretty easily. I've been able to run small errands. I've realized I was definitely using my chair too much. I still need it for trips to big stores, or festivals, or flea markets. Things like that. Right now, I would tire myself out way too quickly without it. It was definitely a test, but it was also an eye opener. I'm proud of myself for how I continue to get over these obstacles. A year ago, I was still confined to a hospital bed. I remember putting all of my energy into wishing I was in the place I am now. I'm up, I'm mobile, I'm living independently. The progress is excellent and still, the work that remains for me is abundant. A year from now, I'd like to be fully out of a chair, with two working arms and hands, and walking with no assistance. A year sounds like so much time but a year ago, where I'm at today seemed unfathomable.

As I read into my journal entries from 2024, I am reminded how inspired and optimistic I was. I really did want to be a new person. I wanted to be better than before my stroke. I remember the buoyancy. I remember feeling filled with optimism and even knowing that I was on a great path. I had all the plans and the motivational speech that I needed, I just didn't have the right motivations. I could talk the talk but I couldn't walk the walk, both literally and figuratively. Part of the choices of my vision board were made hoping they would be enough motivation to keep me focused on my stroke recovery. For instance, love would keep me wanting to heal my weakened body because men like sex and a body that moves easier makes sex better. My book dreams would keep me motivated to heal to make traveling easier. You typically need to travel for a book tour. My vision board had my own apartment on it. I wanted to get better because complete independence would work better with little to no limitations. It seemed like I had a good formula, but I didn't execute it properly.

I spent several weeks only walking on my rollator. Just walking around my hotel room was exhausting. I know that sounds weird, but my good half of my body was carrying the weight of the half of my body affected by the stroke and it also had to be my entire body's strength too. Every step was great for me but it was also energy draining. I was so nervous to travel on my rollator that I spent most days in my hotel. I started feeling trapped at home. I wanted to get out and do something, but just getting there would be exhausting. Add in the mental exhaustion of the event I was going to. My energy drained quickly and I was in desperate need of a wheelchair to travel in. I had just been 'fitted' for a new wheelchair a few days before my wheelchair died. One to fit me specifically. I was waiting on my Medicaid to approve it. This is when I received a letter from Medicaid telling me that they were cancelling my coverage. The cancellation was because I was now receiving income from my disability payments. What they didn't factor in was that I didn't receive my Medicare for another like 17 months. This meant my therapy was going to end, I was not going to get my chair and any progress that could be made from therapy was now going to be paused. I still had some funds left over from my disability backpay. So, I went to the place where everyone went when they needed something for cheap, Amazon. Amazon had a lot of options and I found a new chair that I thought would be perfect. The chair was going to make my life infinitely easier again. I had proven that I could get around on my rollator pretty well, at least around the hotel. I was just easily exhausted. When my chair arrived, I reminded myself that I was on my own in this fight. I took it upon myself to unpack my own chair. I got it unpacked and I built what needed to be built. And I got it put together. The chair measurements from online seemed off and the chair was not what I imagined. I wanted to return the chair, but it was going to be a lot of work and a lot of money, which was running low.

I spoke in my first book about how we are a reactionary system and if we had a proactive system, Medicare would have kicked in sooner, or Medicaid would have continued for longer. The short term coverage could have continued the progress, potentially healing me faster, potentially getting me off of any kind of assistance programs. You know, the socialist programs that regressives complain about and then tell you to pick yourself up by your bootstraps. Those programs. Instead of a proactive approach, I was looking at a 17 month pause of progress. This should make sense to everyone, but we have people that don't see any value in making people better that can get better. At the same time they want to complain about 'drains on the system'. They also want me to get a job using my abilities I do have now. It's much easier to get a job with two working arms and hands, even if I was still in the wheelchair. These are the same people that want to destroy DEIA programs. Yes, D-E-I-A. The A stands for Accessibility. It's always been part of the message of Diversity, Equity, Inclusion and Accessibility. The obstacle was Trump and the heritage Nazis would have had trouble throwing differently abled people under the bus in the beginning. They had to start smaller, so they went after trans people. Either way, this pause was going to be rough but I knew I couldn't let it win.

February 14, 2024

Another Valentine's Day has come and gone for this lonely lady, and probably for the first time in my life my Valentine was me. The one thing I learned from my time in the nursing home was that you don't really need someone to love you. The attention is nice but the only one you need to love you no matter what, is YOU! I have learned that being happy with who you are really does matter more than anything else. I no longer care what anyone else thinks of me, I'm not trying to impress anyone anymore. We are raised to care what others think of us. Our parents, our teachers, the public, but later we're encouraged to ignore it. It's no wonder we are the way we are. We've always been told one thing but expected to do something different. We are taught one thing but supposed to do a different thing. Our brains are pulled in so many directions it's not surprising that we tend to not meet those standards.

I had time to think about this book and the direction I wanted it to go. My first book was my story about what happened after my stroke while I was in the hospital and nursing home. I had so much mentally play out and no one told me anything like that would happen, so I wanted people to know it was normal. In this book, I wanted to continue my story and write about what followed after my discharge. But I'd like it to mean more. I still want it to be the events following my discharge, but I want it to be less like my personal journal and more inspirational. I'd like to provide procedures for dealing with issues rather than just document mine. So if you feel the vibe of the story change, that is the point now. Thanks for understanding.

Call it corny if you want to, but Valentines Day 2024, I chose ME. I always waited to be chosen, I always wanted to be picked. I finally said 'fuck it'. I took Miley's advice and bought myself flowers. I bought myself a nice dinner and some dessert. Afterwards I didn't have to be coerced into something I was not ready for or made to feel bad for not giving up.

February 24, 2024

I took a little break after Valentine's Day to handle some family drama, again. Insert rolling eye emoji here! My family choses my most vulnerable times in my life to show me their asses but while I was vulnerable, I was not weak. They distanced themselves, they failed to keep their promises and they chose to protect an abuser in their circle. When I attempted to hold them accountable, they turned and tried gaslighting me, calling me a mess, crazy and a liar. Their feelings for me were never communicated so I didn't have any ability to talk or work with them. So in respect to my decision to offer more than my story in this book, I will bring up the fact that while we may be communicating our feelings, we can't control how others receive them. As an example, my intentions with the letter I wrote my mother was to bring her to where I was. I spent so long playing and replaying my childhood in my head while I was stuck in a hospital bed, I was put through the trauma all over again, I wasn't going to allow my step father to continue his torment of me, so rather just disappearing on a woman who was vulnerable during her time of illness, I wrote her a letter to explain my distance, she chose to not only be offended and take it personally but chose to share it with others close to me sprinkled with her bias so she could plead her case, I guess, I don't know the intentions of that. Rather than talk about it, they decided to react based on how they interpreted the letter, not off of my intenti-

ons, but off of the information I provided. When we are perceived as one way for so long, changing is like climbing a mountain. People's perception of us becomes us. We lose our autonomy. I could sit around and feel some type of way about my family turning their backs on me but like I said in the letter to my mom, I'm not going to fight for the attention of people that have proven to me that they don't care. It's imprinted on many of us that family comes before anything in life or 'blood is thicker than water', but they can also be the ones that hurt you the worst. So if family is not the healthiest for you or they are proving to be the opposite of a support system, it's ok to let them go. If you're working your ass off to be a better you and they don't want to receive it, then let them go. When you need a cheering section, don't worry about the people ignoring your progress. When we are trying to improve, the last thing we need are people on the inside trying to sabotage us. I'm literally the healthiest I've ever been in my life. I struggled my entire life with over eating. Much of the problem came from the abuse in my past. I assume anyway as over 50% of the people on 'My 600 lbs Life', I turned to food to eat my feelings. When I was lonely or felt like the stereotypical step child or like my mother was choosing her husband over her child, I turned to Little Debbie and second helpings. In my late teens and early 20's I learned to lie to myself about my eating habits, this continued through my early 30's. I tried to change everything in my mid 30's, but my sugar addiction would turn into ravenous hunger and I got into a cycle of eating healthy and then craving sugar so bad, I couldn't go without it. I'd stay awake with hunger pains, because my body would want sugar. My sugar addiction is gone, my portions are controlled, my food intake includes vegetables, my hunger pains have disappeared, this is all very much due to being on dietary restrictions for almost a year, but these are the things I think about when I think about how far I've come. These are all important milestones to remind yourself of when times looks bleak.

THE HARDEST GOODBYE

It was around this time that I was messaged about a Facebook post that my brother posted, offering my dog as a give away. I was never contacted about my dog. I was never allowed to see him when I was in the nursing home. I was furious. I was sad. I was heartbroken. I was flooded with emotions of sadness, anger, more betrayal, loss, all kinds of things. I needed a few minutes of intense crying followed by reasoning with myself. I then decided it was for the best. My baby was rescued from an irresponsible college student who was just going to abandon him. I got several good years of caring for another living being. I spoiled him with monthly grooming baths, paw oiling, and we travelled together a few times.

I took him in the mornings to get him Pup cups and we went for walks. I have fond memories of him running around a local dog park having the most fun. We travelled together all the time, he slept next to me at night. I was in no position to continue to care for a 120lbs fur baby. I adored him and I cried countless tears that he probably felt abandoned again. I always felt terrible that I didn't see him during my recovery, but that wasn't something I could do. In my brother's Facebook post, he called me messy. Why the name calling? I don't know, maybe he felt betrayed in some way. He never spoke his feelings so I may never know why he thought I was messy. Quite honestly, I really didn't care.

I had been growing and maturing the entire time that I was in the nursing home. I had to process my traumas to break through the walls to continue my growth. Being in a hospital bed for over 22 hours a day, you are met with unprocessed, repressed trauma. Your options are to process it, fight to repress it again, or let it consume you. I, sort of, accidentally processed my trauma and worked through it. I wrote it out, I talked it out. I set boundaries and stuck to them. My family didn't know this about me they had not been out to see me very often or they wouldn't hold a long or meaningful conversation with me long enough to recognize those changes in me. Or they saw them and they didn't care. Either way, I had grown. I was different. I had started a journey of self-discovery and healing. I realized through this process that I was walking around a broken person. My stepfather, a "protector", did the very thing he was protecting me from and then after developing a crack in my psyche, he picked at it with his undiagnosed and untreated illnesses and disorders. I'm fairly certain that he suffered daily with ADHD and it wouldn't surprise me to find out if he were on the Autism spectrum. He had a lot of stims. He also has childhood traumas that he hasn't resolved. He would be an excellent candidate for therapy. As I study for my masters in Behavioral Mental Health and Counseling, I recognize so many things from my assigned reading.

I checked out the facebook post and I was processing the emotions I was experiencing. I didn't follow up on what happened to Appa. I just told myself that my brother, even when upset with me, would not give an animal away to harmful people. So, in my mind,

Appa is living a great life, with great humans who also spoil him. He also has animals he lives with that he loves and that love him back. Appa will forever be my fur baby. I will never forget him and I always have pictures of him quickly accessible to me. I even still have a video of him playing with another dog, on my phone. When I miss him, I watch it and I convince myself that he is great and he is living his best dog life.

Appa

The deal with Appa was incredibly final for me. It felt final in many ways. It felt final that I would not see my baby again. It felt final that I may not ever be able to care for an animal again. I didn't want to anyway. I didn't want to be ripped away from my animals ever again. It was incredibly painful. This whole experience made me think about my loneliness and my future. It really started to hit me that I was alone. This was another situation that helped me understand that I really was in this alone. A relationship felt out of the question because not many men want to be in a relationship with a disabled person. Even less want a relationship with a trans woman. Even less than that want a relationship with a person that is iffy about sex. When you add them together you have a disabled, trans woman, with an aversion to sex. My chances of a meaningful relationship with a man is so unlikely that I believe I'd have a better chance of waking up one day and running a marathon with no assistance. I'd love to have the opportunity to do both! When I cried out for help, company or relationships people said that they heard me, but they never really listened. The promises that have been broken are common and many.

I realized that my feeling of loneliness was familiar. When I was in the nursing home, people would come see me once or maybe twice a month. But the rest of my time was filled with conversation with my CNA's or Nurses. I had built friendships with some patients, but nothing like my friends from my pre-stroke life. I now realize that was superficial. When people were face to face with me, I would always drop hints about how I wish more people would text or call. I could always use a visitor. I felt like people would avoid visiting me at the nursing home. Maybe because of the loud noises. Maybe the extra people, or the small close spaces, or the smells. I wasn't sure, but I could understand. When I moved to the hotel, I assumed people would come to visit. Unfortunately, that wasn't the case. I would have to offer food in the hope that my friends would come by and see that I had space and supplies that were suitable for me to have company. I did have a friend that understood that I was free to do coffee dates and they would come pick me up to go out for coffee here and there. Others fell off the radar. I thought I had a bigger support system, but my support system always came equipped with the excuse 'I've just been really busy' or 'work has been a nightmare'. Honestly I understand if that's true, but I still couldn't even get a poop message? That's when you take the time to message someone you don't message often when you are pooping. I couldn't even get a poop message. I honestly started feeling depressed again because of the lack of communication. I was once again realizing that when people find you important in life, they will make time for you. No one was making time for me. I immediately associated that with me not being important to anyone. I was tired of feeling invisible in this fucking world, so I went to the place where everyone is visible, but only if they want to be. I went to Tiktok.

TIKTOK SAVED MY LIFE

As I questioned my value with my people that called themselves friends. I got an idea. I wanted to prove to myself that I could be important to someone. I tested the people that "love' me. I chose to 'fall off the world' for a week. No social media, no outgoing phone calls, No contact with anyone that would tell others that I was alive and well. I waited to see who would reach out to me first. I spent days watching my streaming apps, doing homework and things to occupy my time. I couldn't wait to find out who would be the first one to reach out. Days went by and no one reached out. Everyday I was more hurt than the day before. 8 days later. Not a single person reached out. Not one. If you really want to hurt your own feelings, try the same thing, but honestly I do not recommend it. The way I thought about it originally, I imagined that if I had something happen to me and I died in my sleep, who would find me? Who would alert the authorities? So I decided I would find out who would be the one to discover me.

You would think the people that called themselves your friend would try to call or text people they care about within a week of not hearing from them. By day 8 my body would be rotting and I would only be found because of the smell. I know this is morbid, but I was feeling like I had no value to people in my life. The idea of dying with no dignity was rough on me. My family had already told me that my value was pretty low. Now my friends were telling me that same thing. After 8 days of no sightings, no socials, no contact, no one noticed. I was looking for the person that would be the beacon of light through the fog rolling in. What I didn't anticipate was that there would be no beacon. I expected someone to break through the darkness. For someone to be my light piercing through the dense fog. No one came through. I am the one that broke the experiment. After 8 days, I decided I was done hurting my own feelings. It was incredibly painful to realize that everyone 'loved you', until you realize they actually don't. A few things came to mind when I was upset that my little experiment backfired. First of all, I had set up expectations that people didn't know about. I expected them to think about me when the truth is, I knew that they probably wouldn't. I was never the person that people reached out to randomly. I was never the one that people made plans with. This had certainly not changed since my stroke. I didn't need to do this, but I think this was my version of cutting. The purpose of cutting is to experience a different pain than what is bothering you. The cut signifies a release of those negative or painful emotions. My version of cutting was for me to hurt my own feelings. Sadness was different from loneliness and the difference was enough for one to cut through the other.

When I had my stroke, my Facebook friends were the first to prove to me that our friend status only mattered online. 2,000 people willing to call me a friend online, barely any of them even reached out after my stroke. Further down the road, my family proved to me that I wasn't that important to them. Then my friends gave me 8 long days to realize that I wasn't that important to them either. The part of me that always told me that I didn't deserve love, was laughing and pointing at me. It was upsetting to feel like I still wasn't important to people. I ended up not giving in to my emotions and I decided to look for other friendships. I attempted to get more involved in the hotel community and other community groups local to me. I went to my local disability networking organization and they didn't really host socials to meet other disabled people that might have things in common with you. I tried to get more involved with a job search to maybe try to get back into the job market even at a part time level. I ended up applying for volunteering at a local Loaves and Fishes. While I waited for the background check, I decided to entertain myself on TikTok.

As I was scrolling I came across a couple of TikTok lives that really intrigued me. Some strong women that exuded confidence and political knowledge, blew me away. I was so entertained, educated and engaged that I immediately followed and then she had what she called 'friendly time' at the end of her debate live. I listened to the confidence of people that went up and spoke with passion and conviction. Some of them told personal stories, some of them commented on the MAGA supporters that came up to debate her earlier in the live. She was incredibly knowledgeable and her co-hosts were amazing. It honestly felt like a privilege to watch these people. I felt the community. I felt the love. I felt the comradery. I saw an opening for someone like me. Someone trapped at home, spending days on end alone. I could be a part of a virtual community. I could be a part of the best parts of the internet, because the internet can be an ugly place. I found other creators that were getting hundreds of views on their lives, some were talking about politics, some were talking about their areas of expertise, some were dancing or singing, others were trying to sell me things. I avoided selling lives at all cost, window shopping just reminds me what I can't afford. It was depressing.

Tiktok really became very important to me. Everyday I brought these amazing people into my life. As I gained some courage to fight the stage fright, I started requesting during the 'friendly' portions of lives. I used my sense of humor and my story of tragedy and inspiration to create relationships with people. I was stunned when I found that people actually listened to me. They didn't just listen to me, but they empathized with me. Through time, research, experimenting and content creation, I ended up starting my own lives. It's important to point out that this is when Trump propaganda was increasing daily. The third time Trump ran for president, he spent 4 years criticizing Joe Biden every single day and also hinting at his third run. He said if he lost he would disappear forever, but you know Donald Trump, promises made, promises broken. Every single one of them. I started off in DebateTok. Trying to debate Trump supporters and attempting to sway their voting decision. I realized quickly that Trump supporters were experiencing cult-like cognitive dissonance. They weren't allowed to speak out against Trump, no matter how much evidence was presented to them. They were taught to deny, deny, deny. I also found that when you badmouthed Trump his cult would mass report you for wild shit and my account was banned on several ocassions for days or a week at a time. I gave up on the debating, because the debates always went south. Sometimes literally because these MAGA men on TikTok would go as far as to flash their dicks on TikTok, which would get YOUR account banned or they would end the conversation by yelling the R-slur, the F-slur, the N-slur, which sometimes would also get your account banned. It also went from talking about real issues and real solutions to seeing who could get the other one to crash out first. It was no longer productive, It was just toxic. I got sick of the bans and I started to realize that these people couldn't handle a conversation properly. That is when I ended up creating a good news show called good news tonight. I spent every night discussing good news stories. My hope was that I would attract a crowd that were tired of the bad news stories and people would start to see that even in a world with Donald Trump and Fox news, we could still have stories about good things that were happening in the world. I created a calm environment and we talked about good things happening in the world. I caught on quickly that I was the antithesis of what TikTok wanted. Platforms like that want the drama, the yelling and hot button issues to trigger the algorithm. It wasn't all discouraging. This is when I met a few people that were my favorite people for several months. It felt sudden but out of nowhere, but I found myself with three new girlfriends. I forget the order of how we met, but it was such a quick time between meeting and then bonding. Suddenly, we had a group. There was Cook, Auntie, Kat and Meetri'a. We would constantly message each other and see each other the same lives. It felt like seeing your best friends in school. It escalated quickly from small messages and the occasional drive by shoutouts and it went to meeting up on Discord almost every night. I initially thought I was creating a Discord group for many people that wanted to share information to try and save our democracy. It became much more.

NEW YEAR, NEW FRIENDS

I wanted people to have the opportunity to go somewhere to socialize when they too were feeling lonely in this nation being plunged into fascism. Or if they wanted to learn about new event, information or needed some community. I also wanted to make sure the people were not targeted by predators, especially MAGAs. When you are being vulnerable, MAGA loves to pick at that scab until it becomes a festering, rotting wound. They love using your misery to cause maximum damage. I wanted the safest environment that I could offer for patriots on the left. Believe it or not, we actually don't hate the country. Or babies. We had some different groups meet up a few times, but the Discord meetings turned into the four of us meeting up, some others would join here and there, but typically, it was just us. We had so many conversations and eventually my good news show became our good news show. It was really fun to feel like one of the girls again. In my entire school career, I was always best friends with girls. In high school, I found some girls that let me live open and true to myself, they didn't care that I was a male embracing my feminine side. I was all in for these ladies, but it turned out they were some of the first people in my life to openly say to me that I wasn't worth being friends with. I mentioned in my first book that I spent my graduation alone, that was because these friends of mine terminated our friendship weeks before high school was over. The three of them all cut me off one day, all of them at once. I was deserted. I was waiting for them one morning, waiting at the giant heating and air unit that we always met at and sat on in the mornings. No one showed up! We had been meeting at this unit in the main hall for months. We met in the mornings and gossiped while preparing ourselves for our classes for the day. This was daily and I had no signs that there was a problem. I was left there feeling like I was abandoned. It was a lonely feeling that turned my stomach. I walked the halls that day feeling like I was naked and alone. I was able to just be myself with my friends, without my friends, the experience was much different. It was like those dreams of you getting called on in class and you realize you're naked. I went through the entire day with no sight of, or communication from my friends. I survived the day and went home. The next day one of my friends approached me with a note. She slid the note to me and walked away. There was nothing spoken. Just a note. I didn't save the note, but it was a breakup letter that they all had written together. It hurt me, but this was a thing I always waited for. I grew up hearing that your friends in high school never last forever. I knew that I was going to be the one person that had her high school friends decades after high school.

Well that was a day I feared. I was alone and I didn't have my friends anymore. I was left alone. Alone to face the final weeks of high school and my abusive home life. Clearly this was a painful event for me, because I still reflect on it even today. You see, what I realize now looking back at that friendship is that those girls didn't know it but literally by them accepting me as 'one of the girls', I was receiving gender affirming care from my peers. In high school, I was just living my life as a gay teenage boy. I wasn't 'out', but I was not hiding anything. I didn't know that I wasn't really gay, I knew I wasn't a typical boy. I always knew I was different. I always felt that something was wrong, but I never could pinpoint what was wrong. Unfortunately, my brain was in torment because I was constantly misgendered because I never aligned with being a boy. It was painful to walk to the boy's clothing section, It was hard to go into the 'men's' locker room. I always knew that I was in the wrong place when I was in those places. Those girls accepted me. I look back fondly at them, even after they unfriended me. They were the first ones to accept me and my femininity. It was the first time I didn't need guards up or need to lie about myself with them. My entire life I focused on blending in in a heteronormative manner. It wasn't until my 20's that I developed the ability to not let other people's opinion of me become my problem. I found a way to not care that people hated me. I ignored the haters and started just being myself. Living authentically really pisses them off. This included friends and family too. In my 20's is also when my chosen family came on the scene.

They weren't my only new friends that I made. In 2025, I was really suffering from extreme loneliness and depression. So much so, that I was experiencing the same thing when I was in the nursing home. No calls, no visitors, everyone was busy. I've compared depression to so many things in the course of my writing and I'm going to again. Depression is all of those things. And it has a voice. That voice nags at you. It screams things like
"You aren't good enough!" or

"No one likes you!" or

"No one wants you!" or

"You are alone and always will be!"

Depression says the rudest and most disparaging things. It says horrible shit and because you are vulnerable, you believe them. It hurts and I was considering suicide again. I considered different options and in a moment of clarity, I decided on the best option! I went to a mental health center locally and decided to talk to someone who would listen. I had been through therapy before when I had to go through alcohol recovery after a DUI. I had some therapy also when I was in the hospital after my stroke. The nursing home didn't have regular therapy and that was rough. It felt like a seed of hope had been planted and then it was ripped out of the ground. It sucked. I had suicidal ideations while in the nursing home. Anyone would, to be honest. It is awful there. It feels like death is breathing down your neck. I made the decision to not give in, I fought back. I imagined that the voice was my stepfather. I never wanted him to ever win. I was going to overcome it. I was scared though. I was seriously contemplating different ways to 'self delete'. Sorry, that is my TikTok recommended language coming out. I sometimes can't help it. Considering actual methods and what I would put in my last letter to the world, made me nervous enough to not continue to try it alone. During my intake, it was offered that I would also have a case manager assigned, they would offer a variety of assistance. They offered employment services. I would have the option of therapy and some other programs. It took a little while to get everything started, but it has all been so good. I have loved going through therapy and have even taken a liking to therapy. I went from zero contact from anyone all month to suddenly having contact from others every two weeks. It was nice to feel like people cared. They were paid to care, but they also worked for a community mental health agency, so they did care. It wasn't only about their paychecks it was also about caring for others. I also decided to pick up the usage of their employment services. After my experience volunteering at my local loaves and fishes, I felt that I had a pretty good grip on what kind of accommodations I may need to join the workforce again. I was taught that we needed to have a 9 - 5 job otherwise It wasn't really a job. This is one of those "traditions" we spoke about. With this kind of reasoning being the driving force it was no wonder that Boomers and GenXers were pissed that young people were becoming millionaires from dancing on TikTok.

I was poisoned with this same logic, so I decided to

try whatever I could to get back into the workforce. I knew that working full time was going to be a bear, but I still wanted to try. Living on disability is not the life of lux that people assume it is. It's boring, it's lonely. The money is also shit! I could have spent that time writing, but to write properly I needed the right environment. I could never get comfortable enough to motivate myself to write as much in the nursing home or hotel. .

My Employment Services representative helped me get back into the swing of things, but our efforts were fruitless. I got two solid interviews in housing and both times, I was told that they loved me, but they just stopped communicating quickly. I can't ever say if it was the disability and me in my wheelchair, or the trans woman they saw in front of them, but they did their interviews and then with a hang up of the call, came the end of that option for employment. I was disappointed, but I knew that this world is cruel. And I realized that I needed to make my own way.

PRIDE

My chosen family came to me when a close friend of mine wanted to try drag. We contacted a local drag queen and got a night scheduled to get our faces beat. This was my formal introduction to them. After that our relationship continued to grow. They became my drag family. I would perform with them. I got ready with them nearly every weekend for at least a year. They were the first people I told I was transgender. Eventually they became my chosen family. I trusted them and I confided in them. We learned about each other and we became family.

I recently had an appointment with my therapist and I mentioned how my chosen family taught me how to be myself. They taught me about LGBTQIA+ History and they allowed me just to exist. No walls, no facade. I could just be Meetri'a, unplugged. I wasn't able to be this person around my blood family, I felt I needed to be palletable around them. When I was myself, It always felt like I was being judged. When I disclosed that to my mom, she told me that it was all in my head. I believe I was being gaslit. I'll never not believe that was the case. We have had our issues, but even when we weren't speaking and we were pouring salt in the wounds, we still found each other again. We actually had just reconciled from a dispute we had when I had my stroke. I was fully expecting them to walk away, they didn't have any obligation to me. Our relationship was just recovering. This was a stress that they didn't have to take on. The same way that they were imprinted on me, I guess I was imprinted on them.

Their commitment to my recovery and me in general was one of the things that always brought me back from the brink when my suicidal ideations were screaming in my head. I used it as a tool to survive through the screaming. Suicidal thoughts have a way of feeling like you are in a small room and water is flooding it. The breathing room tightening with every passing minute. I used our relationship as a light to guide me out of that room. I often thought to myself '*Who would mourn my death?*' I would remind myself often that they would miss me. When the thoughts were on the rise, I always defaulted to thinking about them. It was enough for me to want to stick around. I would think of memories of my first time meeting them. I would think all the weekend nights I would be at their house after a night of drag and drinking. I would remember the time we went to Chicago together and had a great time all weekend long. I remembered going to my first market days., my friend pouring a shot into my shoe at The Second Story Bar and I remembered the feelings of being welcomed and wanted. Those are the feelings I reminded myself of, when the water was getting high. My chosen family got through a lot. Chosen family is one the best things we learn about in our community.

Being a member of the 2ALGBTQIA+ community comes with a lot of interesting things. One of the best is Pride. Pride as in living your true and authentic life, but also the annual Pride festival in June. I missed my Pride festival in 2023 because of my mobility issues. By 2024 I was prepared to get back into normal events in my life. I reached out to some friends I hadn't spoken to in a while to see if they would be willing to bring me with them. The only caveat was I needed my chair. My friend came to pick me up and took me down to my local pride festival. I went fully equipped, with all of my necessities and was prepared for a fantastic time in the summer sun with friends, music, colors and queens. We got my chair down to the festival site, not without my friend complaining about how heavy the chair was. I absolutely love when people make me feel like an inconvenience. In fact, I think all differently abled people really like feeling like a huge liability to their friends. We got to the festival just fine and had a wonderful time. I saw a ton of people that I hadn't seen in a long time and spent time with some of them. The beautiful day faded and the sky went dark. The final event of the evening was starting soon. Unfortunately it was delayed. I was supposed to be back by where we had parked the car by 10pm to help my friends work the door of their bar for an after Pride event. I was excited to make a little bit of extra cash. My 'friends' wanted to stay behind to watch the big drag pageant at the end of the festival. I didn't want to fail in my commitment to my other friend's bar. Well the delay of the pageant meant if I wanted to get to the bar next to where we parked to help the bar, that meant I was traveling alone. I have lived in this city my whole life, I had walked home many times and I wasn't afraid.

On my way to the bar, I realized I was not going to make it to the bar before I was going to pee. I stopped at a hotel on the way to the bar. I went into the bathroom and my body was not happy. My bladder released itself before I was ready. I had made a mess of myself. My leggings and underwear were soaked. I didn't want to wheel around smelling like urine so I took off my leggings and underwear. My "top" was two lacy tube tops one black and one pink. I took the one on top and pulled it down to make a skirt and when I got where it was dry, I took my shoes off because they were too soaked. I placed all of my wet clothes in a bag that I had with me. I learned to always carry a 'just 'in case' bag. I was uncomfortable, I was wearing two tube tops to cover my naked body and I went from just wanting to get to the bar, to just wanting to get back to the car. I actually had a change of clothing there. I felt like every passing car saw everything up my makeshift skirt and every passerby knew I was wet with piss. I was absolutely horrified. On the way I called my friend that drove me to see if she could come unlock the car for me, she informed me that she could actually unlock it from her phone anywhere and the pageant hadn't concluded yet so they still hadn't left. I thought all would be fine if only I could make it to the car. It was about 1.1 miles from where we parked by the bar to the festival and I had a wheelchair that could apparently go 15 miles on a charge.

Well I found out the hard way that my chair could probably go that far, on the lowest settings. I wasn't thinking of going slow in my current predicament. About halfway back to the car my battery died on me. I had my charger with me and I had charged my battery sporadically during the festival. I guess it wasn't enough. I sat for a few and turned the chair back on. I scooted about 100 more ft and then she died again. My battery died in front of our local library, however they were closed at 10pm. I looked around for an outlet on the outside of the library, but I saw nothing. I decided it was best to start by calling people. I called the friends I was at the festival with and they were still waiting for the pageant to end. She said they would leave as soon as it ends. I even told them where I was sitting and what happened to me in the bathroom beforehand. That changed nothing. They had no urgency for my situation. I then called my friend's that run the bar by where we parked. I knew they weren't that busy because the crowd wouldn't have been there until after the pageant ended. When I called to ask for help he said there was nothing he could do. I was only alone in this position because I committed to being at his bar to help so I left the group, pissed my pants and now I was literally naked and scared. I sat for like 40 minutes waiting patiently for my friends from the pageant. This is when a person that had walked by me earlier, walked by again. I got a weird feeling and I was not interested in being a sitting duck. I felt like my 'friends' were just not concerned and I was going to be alone in this. I can walk but my left side is incredibly weak and I haven't walked while pushing my wheelchair. I just wanted clothes that were going to cover my privates and I honestly wanted the night to be over. I decided to to walk to the car. I put my piss soaked shoes back on to at least protect my feet. The walk is about .2 miles and roughly 5-7 minutes walking distance. I stood up and slowly started walking myself to the car. Pushing and turning the wheelchair the whole time with one good hand. Step after weakened step. After several breaks to sit down and rest for a few minutes I finally got to viewing the distance of the car. A 5-7 minute walk was easily around 1 hour for me. As the car comes into view I suddenly hear voices behind me. The voices are happy, laughing and completely unconcerned about my wellbeing. It was the people I came with. I was literally a left turn and like 10 feet from the car and one of them asked me if I wanted them to wheel me to the car. I remember rolling my eyes so far into the back of my head, that they almost got stuck. I was angry but also I was in a vulnerable position. So I played kind of nice. I got to the car and was changing my clothes when they started rushing me to get to the bar. That is when I lost it and yelled for them to just go to the bar and I'll get there when I get there. The bar was across the street and a short walk to the entrance. I finally got underwear on and my other clothes were dry now too. I pushed my wheelchair again the rest of the way to the bar and a guy that was outside smoking asked if he could wheel me to the door. I graciously accepted the help of a kind stranger.

When he parked me by an outlet and I plugged my chair in and I broke out into tears. I was finally safe, around people that I knew and I was charging my chair again. I got a small charge on my chair and enjoyed the last few hours at the bar. I wheeled around and talked to some people but mostly spent the evening alone. The feelings of loneliness were strong and I was saddened. I was with people all day, but so alone. This was the night that I fully realized It's only me in this fight for me. I made a similar observation that I made in my first book, but I guess I hadn't applied that logic to all parts of my life. That is a piece of advice I would tell everyone. Regardless of your situation or your particular fight, the only person you can count on in your fight is going to be you. My entire life I was surrounded by people. Did they love me? Or did they love the messiness? My days of popularity were spent being blunt, crass and inebriated. I may have never put my cigarette out on a snarky little queen, if I hadn't had my liquid courage. I may have never thrown a table at someone without the encouragement of the messy ass people egging me on. I was an in-person drama for these realty tv junkies.

When I became a liability I wasn't important anymore. When I finally got home, I collapsed into bed. I was sore for two days. When I jumped online to discuss what happened, my new friends were furious. They couldn't believe that people that called themselves friends were the same people that just abandoned me in the dark city vulnerable to everything. I felt I had suddenly found my new group of girls. Another group of three ladies that expected nothing from me, other than me. They just expected me to just be. We were different ages, we were from different areas and we had different backgrounds. This time, I was an out and proud trans woman and I found my friends again. They made plans to come and see me for my birthday, knowing that no one else would make a big deal out of it! I was looking forward to it. Like most things I've looked forward to in my life, something had to fuck it up. By summer of 2024, Donald Trump's

Nazi rhetoric had been exposed and we knew that if we didn't win the election, this was going to be bad. We knew food was going to be tampered with, we knew he would try to pull back regulations involving breathable air and drinkable water. We knew that jobs were going to be lost and we expected war. The stress was mounting and I was being drained of my optimism. I spent time trying to calm the woes of my friends, but Kat could not ever just prepare for the impact of things she assumed would happen. She had to live in that moment that hadn't happened yet. I honestly was tired of her being an empathy vampire.

An empathy vampire is someone who will suck the empathy out of a person just to have others join them in their misery and they will even manufacture situations to elicit empathetic emotions from those they know will provide them. They suck up that empathy and I don't know if they survive on it, or if it's just like a hit off a drug for the moment only, but that's what I had in my midst. A person that I called a friend was here specifically to feed off of the empathy that I provided. My other friends either failed to see that we had this vampire in our group, or they didn't care. After confronting Kat, I was feeling like I was being avoided again. Suddenly I got a 'note' in the form of a text message. It wasn't what I expected but they decided as a collective that I was a problem and they all called off their association with me. During a live show I was hosting, Kat turned every word of positivity that I said while trying to inspire people to fight forward and get others to get out and vote. She hit my final nerve with her and I finally said *"Fine, Kat! Then lay down and parish, If you feel like your fight is over, then if he gets elected, then just be done!"* I tried to not say lay down and die, but that was the message. I was done! The vampire had sucked all of my empathy and I lashed out. That lash out cost me my friends, again. I got a note slid to me in my text messages and they all walked away. Suddenly they all left my discord and they unfriended or blocked me on everything. They passed me a note and walked away. I was stunned. I was sad but I put together a final good news show. I didn't bad mouth them, I just said we've parted ways, I was sad and even though they had some drama demons spying on me, I still did my show. There were some people that said "bye" and there were some that showed me that they planned on going nowhere. I realized that I had support from 'fans'. I hate the term fan. I prefer community. I was building community. A community where we understand each other. A community where we spoke about politics, American Fascism, all the other isms and we bounced off of each other for inspiration and motivation. So was it New Year, New Friends? Well, yes, just not the friends I thought. The new friends I had were linked through wifi. Does this mean they aren't friends? No, it just means they are a different kind of friend. I got through another abandonment in my life and I was prepped to move on. Good thing too, worse real world problems were rolling in.

MY VERSION OF 107 DAYS

In my first book we talk about my reaction about Hilary Clinton's loss to Trump. In 2024, Joe Biden dropped out of the race and Kamala was named as his successor. The election for Kamala was going to be a fight. She had 107 days to fight years of Trump's rhetoric, lies and division in this country that had been cooking for 10 years. It was an uphill battle from the inception of her presidential run. We all know the results. I was devastated, but I was not surprised. The preview of the misogyny, bigotry and racism that I witnessed on TikTok, I had a feeling that between Elon's admitted tampering and the country still being insanely white man centered, I had a feeling that Kamala was doomed, but I really wanted the country to come through. I will say that I don't do conspiracy theories, but Trump himself said that Elon '*helped*'. Elon said without his 'help' congress would have much different results. Anyway, Kamala losing was huge. Not only was it a huge disruption to my mental health, but MAGA was instructed to poke at that. MAGAs psyop tactics were pretty good, if used on someone susceptible to those mind games. Unfortunately for MAGA I grew up with a stepfather that exhibits every characteristic of a MAGA man. Racism, toxic masculinity, narcissism, a need for control, literally every MAGA man. I've lived a long time with these traits. I know how to block them out or use them to my advantage.

My version of the 107 days of Kamala's historical run for president both started and ended in tears. When the announcement came out that she would run, I cried. I felt the Obama hope all over again. I saw the prosecutor come in up against the criminal billionaire. I wanted so badly for the good guy to win, so I did what I could to help her. I spent the next 107 days following everything Kamala did. Every post, every interview, every townhall. I would take notes and prepare to reley her message.Then I would then go online and discuss what she did to my community, only to watch MAGA deny that it was understandable or coherent. They still to this day use propaganda about her being an alcoholic. This isn't true, the evidence is manufactured and there are still mediocre white people that just don't want to believe that an educated, experienced, black woman could run the country. We had the chance to change the country without the pain of a Nazi-like, fascist takeover or the destruction of countless lives. Unfortunately, it didn't work out that way. We fought, we fought, and we fought, but apparently they needed Trump to hurt and damage our country in order for them to realize what they've done. My entire life growing up, my mother would drop political knowledge on me. She taught me that Democrats were for the working people and Republicans were for large corporations. This was the most basic explanation and has only proven to be true. Republicans have proven that under Trump they could defend sending money to other countries even after screaming '*America First*'.

After the loss, I also cried. I felt, for that day, the Obama-like hope disappeared. Was racism actually too much to defeat? I still wonder this sometimes. I avoided the internet for a few days because the chat bots and the trolls were out in droves to put salt in the wound of those that saw that our country was going to be in turmoil. We spent November to January hoping that Joe Biden was setting up road blocks so that Trump couldn't completely destroy everything. The country was dreading the inauguration. With the exception of the red hat wearing sycophants of a demented old man that seriously threatened over half of the country. It was around this time that I was in a state of heightened emotions. I knew that this would be a good time to write. After my stroke, I wrote a poem about being stalked in the night by a violent assailant. The violent, masked, stalker was the physical manifestation of my stroke. This poem was unfinished and I am not well versed in the art of poetry. I took this premise and expanded the story and wrote a fiction short story entitled Trapped. Trapped is a story of a young woman that was stalked, kidnapped and trapped. It was my first shot at a completed short story. I have included it in this book. Please enjoy.

TRapped

A short story by: Meetri'a Angelo

PART 1 STALKERS

The night was cold. The January wind was like a violently beating on the crowd that night. Nightclubs, restaurants and art galleries were bustling with people enjoying their evening out. The streets were clear of snow but flakes were still dancing in the sky until they gentling hit the ground. A young woman exits CHAOS, a local and popular nightclub. The woman is wearing a cream faux fur coat, a short skirt and heels. When she gets outside she tightens her grip on her coat and begins her short trek home. She gets past the busy part of the strip and disappears fearlessly into the night. On her way home, like many times before, she looks up into the night sky and reflects on the events of the club. She treats the night like a best friend and recaps her exploits. She reminisced about joining her friend in the bathroom and being offered a line of coke. She recalled the the handsome man that bought her a shot at the bar and how it made her feel special. She recounted the other handsome man that hit on her in the coat closet and how he offered her a tablet of ecstasy that caused her to start seeing the most vibrant colors, tasting the club's sounds and feeling the energy vibrating in the room and how it turned into physical euphoria for them both. She felt like she was gliding down the street like she was riding a surfboard. The vibes from the club formed the wave that continued to propel her towards her home. The cold air was sobering and when she rounded the corner she decided that she would never get home without a cigarette to distract her on the walk. She stopped long enough to dig in her purse for a cigarette and her lighter. When she went to light the cigarette, a gust of wind came through, sending chills through her body. Cutting through her. She covered the cigarette from the wind and while taking the initial inhale to get it started. Leaves rustle behind her. Assuming it was the wind, she focused on the cigarette and continued her walk home. She saw her apartment home not too far ahead of her. Through the clicking of her own heels echoing off the houses around her she hears leaves rustling again, only much closer this time. The neighborhood was known for camaraderie, not crime. However, a woman can never be too careful, especially at night and even more so alone at night. The sound of leaves continued to creep her out. So, she moved faster towards her home. Between her momentum and the wind gusting, the blaze of the cigarette was accelerated. The closer she got to her home the closer the noises behind her got. Suddenly the rustling leaves turned into full on footsteps following her. She went into a full on run and made it home quickly. She knew the front door would stick and chose to run behind the apartment house and go through the backdoor. She ran past the telephone pole topped by a flickering street light. Then continued by the front of the building and headed towards the back. The footsteps behind her continued, steady and close. When she got to the backdoor her feet were swept out from under her. The impact of the fall knocked her unconscious. When she came to, her vision was blurry. She reached up and rubbed the back of her head feeling warm blood matting her cold hair. Her vision corrected and she realized that she hit a patch of ice and knocked herself out. She was shaking away the dizzy feeling when she heard the footsteps again. She knew they were close and she had to get to safety. She got up carefully and opened the backdoor into the foyer. She entered quickly, avoiding the patch of ice this time. Once in the foyer, she slammed the door behind her and put her weight against it. She dug in her purse, looking for her keyring. The apartment building had a front and back door that remained unlocked, those led into foyers. Then, there were locked doors that led into a hallway that had rows of apartment doors on either side. While looking for her keys, the door handle on the backdoor began to turn and jiggle. This turned into pushing and shaking. She started to panic and felt only a sliver of relief when she found her keys. She leaned forward and struggled to get the key into the lock. Suddenly, someone started pounding on the door behind her. As the key finally slid in, she was able to gather her nerves and knew safety was only a key turn away. She turned the key, waiting for a click. When the lock finally opened, she knew salvation was close. She threw the hallway door open and leapt into the hall, quickly closing the foyer door behind her. When she turned the lock to secure the door, she looked in the window and saw the backdoor's handle turn, then the door slowly swung open. When the door opened a figure stood in the doorway wearing all black with a mask that had a neon yellow smile with neon yellow X's for eyes. Seeing her stalker face to face sent her into a heightened state of panic and she ran a few doors down and found apartment 11. She fumbled to find her apartment key on the ring she was still holding. When she found her apartment key the same scene replayed. She struggled to get the key in the lock. Just then, there was a tapping at the back window. Her curiosity took over and she looked back at the window. The stalker was now holding a large menacing hunting knife which he used to tap the glass. He was pointed at the door on the other end of the hall, where the front door was. There in the front door's window stood another figure wearing the same dark clothing and the same mask, attempting to get into the front door. Caitlin screamed a blood curdling scream! She fought through her rising panic to get into her apartment. The feeling of being trapped in this hallway was overwhelming. The keys fell through her shaky hands. She grabbed the ring off of the floor and found her apartment key again and slid it into the lock. When she swung her front door open she immediately felt safe. She quickly moved inside, closed the door and locked all of the locks.

PART 2 INVASION

Once she had secured the locks, the woman slid down the wall, leaving a blood trail from her head wound. When she reached the floor she laid her head on her knees and began to cry. As her anxiety calmed down a bit, she was so overwhelmed by the experience and the tears started flowing. Suddenly, she heard glass break in the hallway, she stood up quickly, then turned around to check the locks again. Her anxiety returned when her door handle was jiggled and someone started pounding on the door. The pounding got increasingly more aggressive and the girl screamed out through the anxiety and tears.

"Leave me alone!" she cried.

"Answer the door, I just want to make sure you're alright!" The man's voice was deep and menacing.

"Leave me alone!" she screamed again!

The pounding continued and the terror continued mounting.

"I'm calling the police!" she screamed with panic in her voice.

Suddenly the pounding on the door stopped. The silence became deafening. Just calm nothingness.

"Caitlin. Open the door. We want to help you." A woman's voice broke the silence.

"How do you know my name?" Caitlin asked, terrified.

The door handle was being jiggled again and Caitlin screamed out! She grabbed her phone out of her purse and dialed 9-1-1. The operator picked up. "What is your emergency?"

"Please help! I was followed home and they are trying to break into my apartment. Please send the police!" Caitlin explained pleading for help.

"Caitlin, open the door. They just want to help you." the operator's voice changed.

Caitlin was left speechless. How did they intercept her call? What was happening and why was she involved? She was distracted by all of the unknowns swirling around her. Suddenly, there was a forceful kick on the door. So forceful, it knocked her forward and she dropped her phone. A second kick and the door sprang open. The wood frame splintered and the only thing holding the door closed were a few chains. A black gloved hand appeared inside the door grabbing for the locks. Caitlin screamed again.

"She's got the chain locked." the same woman yelled out, informing the others.

Caitlin scrambled to her feet, using quick thinking she ran into her kitchen. She reached her knife block and every single knife was gone.

"Fuck!" She screamed not believing this situation.

She went to the sink, which was full. In her panic she began tossing the dishes on the floor looking for anything to use as a weapon. The sink was filled only with plastic cups and plates. No knives, no heavy pans, not even a fork. Once again, she was confused.

"Where did my stuff go?" She asked herself.

Just then she heard another kick at the door. She panicked and ran to her bedroom and slammed the door behind her. She pushed her dresser in front of the door to block it and she went digging for a weapon. She checked the closet for her fiancé's sporting equipment. Once again, nothing! No golf club, no baseball bat, no tennis racket. When she heard the front door chain giveaway with another kick, shepanicked. She knelt down to the floor and reached under the bed and pulled out a metal box. She typed in 11323 on the keypad and it lit up green and clicked. She opened the box and pulled out a gun she had never used!

"You got this Caitlin!" She reassured herself.

She cocked the gun confirming it was loaded and prepared for the barricaded door to be attacked. She sat on the edge of the bed waiting as the anticipation mounted. She listened for any commotion outside of the bedroom. Once again, silence filled the entire apartment. Nothing at all. No noise from the other side of the door. Suddenly afamiliar tapping on her bedroom window, like the tapping made from the hunter's knife on the glass earlier. Caitlin's curiosity sent her slowly across the room to investigate. She parted the blinds to peak outside. The flickering street light could be seen illuminating the darkness, yet it revealed nothing. Caitlin released the blinds and went to head back to the bed. When she turned around, there stood one of the stalkers holding a baseball bat. He swung quickly and connected with Caitlin, knocking her out cold.

When Caitlin woke up, her head hurt and her vision was blurry. She tried lifting her arm to rub her head, but her arm was strapped down to the bed. Through the blurry vision she could only see a very bright white room.

"Am I dead?" she asked herself.

It took some time but when her eyes adjusted she could finally see that she was indeed in a white room made out of cement blocks. The white of the room was intensified by bright white lights, It was kinda like looking at the sun too long. Caitlin looked around the room to avoid the burning light. The walls were bare and cold. The only windows were on the same wall as the door and looked into what appeared to be a stark white hallway. Caitlin looked down and saw that her clothes had been removed and she was now wearing what looked like a hospital gown. Her arms and legs were strapped down with thick, heavy, worn, leather straps with huge buckles. Caitlin tried moving to see if there was any give, but the straps wouldn't budge. Looking out the window, Caitlin saw a woman walking by, no mask and dressed in all white.

"Help!" Caitlin screamed through a weakened holler. She was hoping the woman would do something to help her, but the woman continued to walk down the hall. This told Caitlin that the woman couldn't or wouldn't hear her. Keeping her eyes on the window, hoping that someone else would come by, or the woman would come back. Suddenly a masked person dressed in black came walking by the window. The person turned to face Caitlin and they were also wearing the mask with the neon yellow x's and smile like the ones at her apartment.

"No!" Caitlin howled in agony.

They then put their hands up, as if they are shocked by the shriek. They put one hand in front of their mouth and the other pointing at Caitlin. Their shoulders started moving up and down, as if they were laughing at her. Caitlin started crying and as if she was praying she says "Please help me!" The desperation is thick in her voice as she makes a plea through her tears. The figure walks out of view and Caitlin is left only with unanswered questions, mounting fear and massive anxiety. She wondered how she will escape from being trapped in this room.

PART 3 BOUND

Caitlin lays there for what feels like hours, randomly trying to move anything she could, but the straps wouldn't budge an inch. She periodically cried out for help but no one ever came. Caitlin was on the verge of just giving up and letting whatever that was going to happen just happen. It was then that Caitlin heard an all too familiar tapping on the window. She looked to see if it was another masked figure. She was not surprised when she saw one of them. She was shocked when she saw five of them. They were all watching her through the window. They were wagging their knives or waving, or pointing and laughing. The torment was unbearable, but when you are strapped to a bed, helpless, all you can do is close your eyes. So that is what she did. She closed her eyes and thought of better times. She heard the door to her room open and that is when she realized they were entering her room. She thought the adrenaline alone would kill her. Her body stiffed from the tension and her muscles began to vibrate the tight straps keeping her firmly in place.

"Oh God! Help me!" She wailed.

The five figures surrounded the bed. Caitlin was shaking from her fear. She didn't understand what was happening. Four of the figures unstrapped her and then grabbed the limb that they unstrapped and started moving it around with no rhyme or reason, but they kept moving them. The fifth one pulled out what would have been a comically large syringe. However, this was not funny to Caitlin.

"You might feel a pinch!" the masked figure jokes in a clownish tone.

She screeched in pure dread again. She also discovered that even though her limbs were free, she still had no control over them or strength to move them. The fifth figure stuck the needle into her arm as another held her arm in place. She watched her blood gushing into the syringe as they pulled the plunger. She wondered if she even had that much blood in her body. She closed her eyes tight and started sobbing. Suddenly, she felt nothing. No needle, no one messing with her arms or legs, there was no presence in the room. She opened her eyes and the bright light above the bed seared into her retinas again. She looked down and noticed the straps swinging on the side of the bed. Caitlin tried sitting up but found that she was incredibly weak.

"They must have drugged me. Or maybe they took all of my blood." She whispered to herself, questioning her weakness.

She also questioned how the room was suddenly vacant. She didn't remember passing out. The curious events continued to pile up. Just then the woman from earlier was back in the hallway. She was dressed in all white like a nurse from the 50's. She wore a boxy hat with a Red Cross on it. She entered the room and approached Caitlin's bed.

"Time to eat!" The nurse was cheery and had a Mary Poppins' disposition.

"Thank God you're here, please help me!" Caitlin's desperation was clear in her voice while she whispered to the nurse.

The woman acted as though she couldn't hear her. She pulled a cart in the room with what looked like a thick milkshake on it and a funnel. The nurse pulled Caitlin's shirt up revealing a tube coming out of her stomach.

"What is that? What have you people done to me?!" She hollared at the nurse repeatedly and not even a flinch.

The nurse connected the funnel and poured the milkshake substance into the funnel.

"Please help me, please!" Caitlin's bottom lip quivered with her emotional plea.

The nurse made eye contact with her.

"You're the only one that can help yourself out of this!" The nurse said with an annoyed tone.

As the nurse left her room, the door closed behind her and Caitlin's frustrations were peaking as she started weeping again. Just then the five masked figures popped up and were taping on the window, again.

"It's up to you Caitlin. It's all up to you!" They all repeated in unison.

"What's up to me?" Caitlin yelled in her best weakened effort, begging for answers.

Another woman in 50's nursing garb came into her room and she was holding a tablet of some kind. She pressed a button on the screen and the tablet started making a ringing sound. A man comes on the screen.

"Hello, Caitlin!" The man greeted her.

GREG!" She bellowed when she saw her fiance. "Greg, get me out of here!" Caitlin begged.

"Caitlin, it's all up to you, honey! You know that." Greg reiterated the same thing she's been hearing.

"What's going on? Where am I?" Caitlin demanded to know, just then the woman coldly took the tablet away and walked out of the room.

Caitlin howled as the woman walked out the door. "GREG!"

Caitlin laid there for the next few hours staring at the ceiling, blubbering the whole time. Caitlin didn't know what to do. She couldn't see any way out of this situation. She was free from those straps, but she still couldn't move. The people that did interact with her didn't help her in any way. Her fiancé must know she's here and he's not helping her. But where is "here"? She doesn't even know where she is or what's happening to her. She was scared and couldn't understand what the hell was going on. Who was stalking her earlier? Who are these people in the masks? Why is there a tube in her stomach, what does her fiancé have to do with it? She had 1,000 questions and no answers. There was no clarity between the anger and the confusion.

Suddenly a man entered the room with an empty wheelchair. He is dressed in jeans and a plan t-shirt.

"Alright. It's your turn. You're coming with me!" When he touched Caitlin, her body shuttered in fear.

The man giggled and apologized at the reaction. He then helped Caitlin sit up in bed. This felt so good, to finally be sitting upright, but did not change her level of fear from her situation. The man threw her arm around his shoulders and helped her stand up. Her legs were very weak and were buckling under her weight, but he was holding her up and he wouldn't let her fall.

"They drugged me!" She pointed out, weakened by the draining events.

The man brushed off the comment, slightly offending her, but if the worst he did to her was offend or ignore, she would be ok with that. She was so vulnerable right now and she was in no position to fight.

"Where are we going?"' She asked him as he helped her and her weakened legs shuffle her feet to the wheelchair.

Again, she was ignored. The man still had a hold of her to make sure she wouldn't fall. He helped her turn around and lowered her into the seat. He put her feet on the footrests and then stepped behind her and pushed the wheelchair out of the room. Caitlin was still terrified but she was out of her restraints and she was leaving the room. She was both terrified and happy and that was boggling to her. It was a strange cocktail of emotions, but she felt like there was hope for her. She still had no idea where she was or how she got here or how she would get out, but she was at least getting a layout of this place. As the manwheeled her out in the hallway, she immediately started making mental notes of building details. The man wheeled her around a corner and ahead of her was a dark hallway with a dim flickering light at the end of it. There were streams of light coming through the windows along the hall that were looking into the rooms, but with no overhead lighting, the hall was quite eerie. While quickly wheeling Caitlin down the hallway, the man stopped suddenly. "I'll be right back." He said with a friendly and polite tone.

The man left Caitlin alone in the hallway and entered another room for a quick visit. Caitlin watched the man start talking to someone out of view, Caitlin heard a familiar sound. Heavy footsteps approaching behind her.

PART 4 SOMETHING SINISTER

As she started to panic again, she tried lowering her

arms to move her wheelchair, she believed the drugs were keeping her weak still. She whimpered as her fear got the better of her. Caitlin couldn't hold it back anymore and she screamed out loud, in the middle of her scream, she felt her bladder release and her seat got very warm. Tears streamed down her face while urine ran down her legs. Through the sound of liquid splashing to the ground and whimpers, the footsteps were getting closer. Just then, out of her tear flooded peripheral she saw a large figure dressed in all black wearing that mask like the others. The man is somehow able to smoke a cigarette through the mask and he takes a long drag off of the cigarette. He exhales the smoke, also through the mask, and throws the cigarette on the ground. He stomps it out as the cloud of smoke travels down the hall. From a sheath on his side, he draws a familiar and large hunters knife. It's long and the sharp blade glistens in what little light is penetrating the darkness from the room the polite man was in. Caitlin starts whimpering and the kind man appears in the window with a random woman standing next to him. She is dressed in a similar hospital gown as Caitlin. Suddenly the knife wielding man appears in the room.

"He's in there with you!" Caitlin screams.

How did they not notice him? Somehow with neither of them alerted, the masked man grabs the woman by the hair on top of her head. He pulls her head back and the woman tries to scream out, but her scream is silent. The masked man puts the knife to the woman's throat and quickly drags the sharp blade across it. The wound opens wide and blood pours out. The woman looks at Caitlin as though she were asking for help. She grabs at her throat to presumably stop the bleeding. The wound is extreme and she quickly succumbs to it. The woman's eyes roll into the back of her head and she collapses, falling out of view. Caitlin closes her eyes tight through the tears, unable to watch anymore of this. With her eyes still closed she hears footsteps again. Suddenly she feels a hand on her shoulder. She jumps and shrieks out in horror.

"You ready?" Asked the friendly calming voice from the polite man.

She looked up at him with terror in her eyes. She wondered how he was ok and why wasn't he concerned by what just happened. He smiled big at her with a beautiful toothy smile. He began wheeling her down the hall again. He was humming some unrecognizable, happy tune while he pushed her.

Why was he so unbothered by what just happened? A woman was murdered next to him! Caitlin was on the edge of breaking. She felt like something far more sinister was going on. As the chair is being driven past the next room, another masked figure comes out of the door, wiping blood from his knife. The room smelled of stale cigarette smoke. The window of the room was covered in bloody handprints. Caitlin was wheeled by it like nothing was wrong. The light at the end of the hall continues to flicker. The next room had a masked man kneeling on the bed, shoving needles filled with dark liquid into a man's arm. The man pushes the plungers, plunging the drug into his veins. The man seizes and foams at the mouth. The masked man looked at Caitlin and put his hands in front of his mouth like he was laughing again. They continued down the hall. The man continued to be unfazed by what was happening in front of them. Caitlin was petrified. A room a few doors down was another scene. A man stood in the doorway drinking whiskey out of the bottle. A masked man was stalking him from behind. Suddenly, the giant blade popped out of his chest, splattering the two with blood. The masked man kicked the dead man off of his knife and he fell to the ground. Caitlin was convinced she was being driven to the slaughter, and started sobbing uncontrollably.

"Why are you so upset? We are gonna have fun!" said the polite man, Enthusiastically ominous.

When they reached the end of the hall they were

under the flickering light, they turned into an open door. The room was calm and felt inviting. There was no sign of the masked figures, no blood, no screams. This looked like a small gym. There was small equipment, mirrors, exercise balls and dumbbells.

Somehow her terror faded away and she was comfortable. She felt safe . Her tears began to dry and her anxiety melted away. Things were very strange, but the rollercoaster of emotions was overwhelming.

"What was that?" She asks not sure what that happened in the hallway.

"Where am I?" Caitlin tries talking to the man again.

His frustration takes over and his big smile fades quickly into pursing lips as he ignores her. The man parks the wheelchair by the back wall in the room and he bends down to lock the wheel breaks. He moves to the front of her and helps her stand up, it was easier for her this time. She felt like the drugs were wearing off. In an effort to remain subtle, she tested her fingers by giving them a slight wiggle. The man propped her up against the wall and let go of her. She stood there, stable, with her shoulder against the wall.

"Ok, you feel strong? Just stand here for a few minutes, I'm gonna get towels and a change of clothes to clean up your mess." The man sounded snarky with her, but she still felt like she might have a shot to get away.

Caitlin watched the man leave, and was still confused with everything. The man walked away from her saying nothing else. She's used to it now. When the man walks out the door, Caitlin looks around the room and in front of her she sees a door she hadn't noticed initially. Putting any strength into it that she could, Caitlin tries walking towards the door. To her astonishment she was able to walk again with very little weakness. The drugs seemed to have worn off. She moves to the door and she is able to open the door. Suddenly, there is a tap on the window in the door to the room. A noise she now knows well.In the hallway stands one of the masked men tapping a bloody knife against the glass. "Did he kill the polite man?" she wondered to herself. Caitlin runs into the doorway to escape the masked man again.

PART 5 GLITCh

On the other side of the doorway she walks into a bathroom stall. Her wet hospital gown has somehow changed back to her dry club clothes and her heels are back on her feet, red toes and all. "Caitlin! Finish your line!" Caitlin hears a familiar voice behind her through the thumping bass.

Behind her she finds a woman with long black hair pointing to a line of cocaine prepared neatly for her on the top of the tampon disposal box next to the toilet. Caitlin leans down to do her line and when she stands back up, sniffling strongly to inhale any residual, her dark haired friend is now masked in the same mask that's been terrorizing her.

She is holding that familiar hunters knife. The dark-haired woman suddenly lunges at Caitlin with rage. Caitlin jumped out of the way, kicked the stall door open and ran out of the bathroom in a panic. Immediately she feels safe again when she's out in the bar area. The music seems to wash away the terror and she goes back to normal business. "I need a drink!" She says to herself exhausted. She walks to the bar almost by instinct and hanging on a seat next to her is her faux fur coat. She takes a seat and puts her head in her hands and starts talking to herself. "Caitlin, what the fuck is happening right now?" Caitlin asks herself out loud and just wanted to wake up or snap out of it. Whatever was happening, this was a nightmare and she couldn't take it anymore.

Caitlin was so confused and she chose to rely on the idea that if this was a delusion, she was at least not stuck in a room anymore. If this wasn't a delusion then she would figure it out later. As she sat trying to make sense of what was real, she was interrupted.

"Miss!" A man called out to her from the other side of the bar. When Caitlin looked up the bartender, resembling the polite man, was holding a shot out for her.

"This was bought for you." He said, setting the shot out in front of her.

"Where is this coming from?" She asked the bartender.

"That man down there." The bartender pointed to a man at the end of the bar.

Caitlin expected to see another masked man when she looked but it was not, it was a very handsome man with a huge grin. He raised his shot, encouraging her to also raise her glass. So she does, with a clink in the air and a tap on the bar for good luck they oth took their shots. As Caitlin puts her empty glass down and pushes it to the end of the bar, she keeps her eyes on the man that bought her a shot. Suddenly, the man next to her stabbed a familiar and giant hunting knife into the bar. When he turned around he was wearing that mask again. Caitlin nearly tripped, jumping out of her seat so quickly. She grabbed her coat and ran to the front door. She got roughly 50 feet away from the bar, and as quickly as the terror set in, the calm came washing over her and her run slowed to a sexy walk matching the beat of the club music. She continued to walk towards the exit and as she passed the coat closet. A man exited the closet and ran into her. She stumbled but stayed on her feet. As she gathered herself, she saw that an attractetive, dark haired man ran into her. Her heart began pounding, but not from fear. From attraction.

Do you want me to put your coat away?" The man asked, smiling a smile that was melting Caitlin. She held her coat and was lost in this man's eyes.

"You're not leaving, are you?" The man asked, a bit hurt by the notion.

Caitlin realized she needed to respond. She was leaving, and she did need to go home, but the music, the liquid and chemical influences were a perfect recipe to convince her to stay.

"I'm not leaving. Thank you for offering." Caitlin responded coyly and while handing over her coat, she forgot about worrying that she was still in a bar with at least two two masked pyschopaths.

It felt like she was on autopilot. He hung the coat up and looked back at Caitlin. He turned to her, put his hands in his pockets and in doing so, he pulled his jeans down enough to expose the beginning of his defined V-cut and some dark pubes intensified against his pale white skin. He pulled a small baggie out of his pocket and made an x with his fingers to indicate the offering. Caitlin stepped into the closet and took the baggy. She opened it and popped the pill. Deciding to take her chance she grabbed the man's head and kissed him. Not missing his opportunity he kissed her back. He held her body close to his. The heightened senses caused the kissing to escalate. She reached in his pants and he reciprocated. As he grew in her hand, he found his target causing her to moan loudly. She was roughly pushed against hanging coats as he pushed into her body with his, causing them to fall. The sounds that were coming from the coat closet alerted security.

"Hey! Ya'll gotta get out of here!" A security guard barked at them, indicating to get out of the closet.

Embarrassed and sobered, Caitlin grabbed her coat and made her way to the exit door. Caitlin swung her coat around and slid her arms into the sleeves. She hugs her coat tight and leaves the club.

The night was cold. The January wind was like a violently beating on the crowd that night. Nightclubs, restaurants and art galleries were bustling with people enjoying their evening out. The streets were clear of snow but flakes were still dancing in the sky until they gentling hit the ground. A young woman exits CHAOS, a local and popular nightclub. The woman is wearing a cream faux fur coat, a short skirt and heels. When she gets outside she tightens her grip on her coat and begins her short trek home. She gets past the busy part of the strip and disappears fearlessly into the night. On her way home, like many times before, she looks up into the night sky and reflects on the events of the club. She treats the night like a best friend and recaps her exploits. She reminisced about joining her friend in the bathroom and being offered a line of coke. She recalled the the handsome man that bought her a shot at the bar and how it made her feel special. She recounted the other handsome man that hit on her in the coat closet and how he offered her a tablet of ecstasy that caused her to start seeing the most vibrant colors, tasting the club's sounds and feeling the energy vibrating in the room and how it turned into physical euphoria for them both. She felt like she was gliding down the street like she was riding a surfboard. The vibes from the club formed the wave that continued to propel her towards her home. The cold air was sobering and when she rounded the corner she decided that she would never get home without a cigarette to distract her on the walk. She stopped long enough to dig in her purse for a cigarette and her lighter. When she went to light the cigarette, a gust of wind came through, sending chills through her body. Cutting through her. She covered the cigarette from the wind and while taking the initial inhale to get it started. Leaves rustle behind her. Assuming it was the wind, she focused on the cigarette and continued her walk home. She saw her apartment home not too far ahead of her. Through the clicking of her own heels echoing off the houses around her she hears leaves rustling again, only much closer this time. The neighborhood was known for camaraderie, not crime. However, a woman can never be too careful, especially at night and even more so alone at night. The sound of leaves continued to creep her out. So, she moved faster towards her home. Between her momentum and the wind gusting, the blaze of the cigarette was accelerated. The closer she got to her home the closer the noises behind her got. Suddenly the rustling leaves turned into full on footsteps following her. She went into a full on run and made it home quickly. She knew the front door would stick and chose to run behind the apartment house and go through the backdoor. She ran past the telephone pole topped by a flickering street light. Then continued by the front of the building and headed towards the back. The footsteps behind her continued, steady and close. When she got to the backdoor her feet were swept out from under her. The impact of the fall knocked her unconscious. When she came to, her vision was blurry. She reached up and rubbed the back of her head feeling warm blood matting her cold hair. Her vision corrected and she realized that she hit a patch of ice and knocked herself out. She was shaking away the dizzy feeling when she heard the footsteps again. She knew they were close and she had to get to safety. She got up carefully and opened the backdoor into the foyer. She entered quickly, avoiding the patch of ice this time. Once in the foyer, she slammed the door behind her and put her weight against it. She dug in her purse, looking for her keyring. The apartment building had a front and back door that remained unlocked, those led into foyers. Then, there were locked doors that led into a hallway that had rows of apartment doors on either side. While looking for her keys, the door handle on the backdoor began to turn and jiggle. This turned into pushing and shaking. She started to panic and felt only a sliver of relief when she found her keys. She leaned forward and struggled to get the key into the lock. Suddenly, someone started pounding on the door behind her. As the key finally slid in, she was able to gather her nerves and knew safety was only a key turn away. She turned the key, waiting for a click. When the lock finally opened, she knew salvation was close. She threw the hallway door open and leapt into the hall, quickly closing the foyer door behind her. When she turned the lock to secure the door, she looked in the window and saw the backdoor's handle turn, then the door slowly swung open. When the door opened a figure stood in the doorway wearing all black with a mask that had a neon yellow smile with neon yellow X's for eyes. Seeing her stalker face to face sent her into a heightened state of panic and she ran a few doors down and found apartment 11. She fumbled to find her apartment key on the ring she was still holding. When she found her apartment key the same scene replayed. She struggled to get the key in the lock. Just then, there was a tapping at the back window. Her curiosity took over and she looked back at the window. The stalker was now holding a large menacing hunting knife which he used to tap the glass. He was pointed at the door on the other end of the hall, where the front door was. There in the front door's window stood another figure wearing the same dark clothing and the same mask, attempting to get into the front door. Caitlin screamed a blood curdling scream!

PART 6 TRAPPED

"Who keeps screaming?" A young woman asked an

older woman as they walked side-by-side down a bright white hallway. The hallway is lined with doors and windows. Each door enters a different patient's room and in between the doors are windows into the rooms. Some patients were hooked up to feeding tubes, others to breathing machines and other assistive medical machinery. The two women turn a corner and start down a different hallway.

"This is our Specialty Care Stroke Wing. Everyone down this Hall has suffered a massive stroke and their recovery is either not going to happen or it's taking longer than anticipated. They've been deemed to need special care. This young lady here is Caitlin. She's our resident screamer!" The woman stops and points to the young woman lying in bed in room 11.

"She is one of our most unique cases. She had recently turned 36." The experienced CNA explains to the new CNA.

"Wait! Did you say 36?" The new CNA asked.

"Yes, 36." The older, experienced woman confirmed.

"She had a stroke that young?" The younger new CNA was dumbfounded.

"Yes. From what they pieced together she was walking home from the club by her apartment and got spooked by something, so she started running home. She slipped near her back door and hit her head causing a brain bleed. She alerted people both inside and outside of the building, screaming about being chased. A random passerby tried to enter her building to help her but she slammed the door on him. He broke the building window to get in to help her, by then she was in her apartment with her door locked. Her upstairs neighbors tried getting in to check on her, but she wouldn't open the door even for them. She called 9-1-1, dispatch tried to get her to open the door, but she wouldn't. They finally kicked the door in, but the chain lock would not come unlatched. They watched her run to her kitchen then into her bedroom where they found her, she collapsed while trying to get a tennis racket from under her bed. Two days later she woke up here. The stroke had taken effect and the bleeding caused damage to both sides of her body so all of her limbs were weakened. She opens her eyes and looks at you but she'll just scream or yell for help. We remind her that it's up to her to regain control of her limbs. She has to remind her brain that she's in there. She looks like she sees you, but we think she sees you very differently. Like she is hallucinating images." The experienced CNA explains.

"That is wild! One slip and your whole life could be turned inside out, huh?" The new CNA asked very curious.

The slip caused the immediate brain bleed, but her bloodwork showed traces of nicotine, alcohol and different drugs. Her blood pressure and blood sugar were both very high. One of these factors can cause a stroke, she had five. She was clearly not taking care of herself and strokes don't care about your age, social status, or money. When you combine so many bad factors in the same body, you're asking for it. You invite your own deadly stalker in." The experienced CNA tried to educate and warn the young CNA.

"Anything else I should know about her?" The younger CNA asked, still curious about Caitlin's predicament.

"It's hard to say, we know the physical effects of her stroke but the mental effects are a mystery like with any other brain injury. Because of the repeating of the same phrases and the precise timing between them, doctors believe that she is trapped in a loop of reliving memories with lucid moments mixed in. Like when she sees her fiancé, Greg, in video chats. Those conversations are always different. Sadly every time he hangs up, she resets and the scenario she is living in her head continues. The lucidity ends with the call, or the visit. Greg stayed up here for a week one time because doctors saw that he breaks her out of her loop when he calls in. He stayed in her room and she spent the whole week in conversations with him. Remembering memories of the two of them together. She was like a whole different person. When he left to go back to work, she resetagain."

"So, have they given up on her?" The new CNA asks, now enamored by this woman.

"No, her brain could release her at any time and she could recover, but until then we keep her alive. She is part of a case study for this place. They monitor everything about her daily and report it. They check her weaknesses, they take her bloodwork, occasionally therapy wheels her down to their office, but she tries to run away. One day she could snap back, but until then she is trapped in some hell that her mind created. We are all one accident away from this.

THE END

NOW, BACK TO YOUR
REGULARLY
SCHEDULED
PROGRAMMING

STARTING A NEW CHAPTER

Getting this story out of me was a huge relief. It's a funny thing, but emotionally charged art is always the best. Feeling the need to write when you have built up stress or anxiety is interesting because whatever you need to write to alleviate those emotions can also cause those same emotions. Writing Trapped was stressful because I wanted to hit every pain point from my experiences after the stroke. I also wanted to offer an entertaining read while expelling those negative emotions. I think I did well and that short story ignited my fuse for me to start my first full fiction novel. I am working on that now as well. Check my website for more details. Pardon the shameless plug. But also meetriaangelo.com.

After my stroke, I had visions of being stalked by a vicious assailant. I was completely ignoring the things that actually threatened my life. In my first book, I talk about spiraling. I sometimes say that the universe pumped my brakes for me with my stroke. It could have been so much worse. The version of my stroke that I had was extremely dense and has been difficult to overcome, but I could have been one of the victims of a stroke, where all of my mobility was taken, or my ability to speak at all. I spent 10 months roaming the halls of a nursing home where I felt I was ignored or tormented by forces that no one could see. I saw people using their eyes to communicate their stories. Some begging for help, some replaying a previous life from their memories on repeat. I was able to memorialize some people in my story and I have so many easter eggs in 'Trapped'. I got to put personal memories from the nursing home in it. Albeit in a gruesome manner, but memories nevertheless.

Part of wanting to write 'Trapped' was the heightened emotions, part of it was having a story to tell, the other part was me testing my fiction writing abilities. While I spent my days scrolling TikTok, connecting with internet friends that seemed to adore me. I used that same group as a test to see how they reacted to my fiction writing. They seemed receptive and I was prepared to go full steam ahead.

I recall around this time I went to pay my monthly rental rate to the hotel and for that month the price suddenly shot up nearly $500. Being on a fixed income, this wasn't doable. I was never going to make up that amount so quickly. And if I was going to end up on the streets. I'd never make it. I was offered the homeless shelter as an option when I was leaving the nursing home. I looked into it and it wasn't an option for me. I wouldn't survive on the streets with no protections. I wasn't going to survive without a stable living environment. I left one temporary home in the nursing home for a different temporary home in the hotel. The steep increase in price was one of the things I was trying to avoid when I asked my mother to help cosign an apartment for me. I was already paying between $850-$1500 for a hotel room per month for almost two years.

The walls of the hotel room were suddenly incredibly familiar. I had had a great training space to practice living independently. I cooked for myself, did my own laundry, showered on my own, cleaned my own messes. I made and kept my own appointments. I was living an independent life no different from anyone else, but I needed an apartment of my own. Specifically for a place that was mine, a true place to call home, but also because a lease would lock me into a price for at least 12 months. I had averted the crisis that month, but now I was thoroughly terrified for my future. This is when the demand for my own space really fired up. I had proven that I could live on my own without constant supervision or even the occasional check in from the hotel's friendly maintenance man or front desk attendant. It was funny when I wouldn't make an appearance for a few days around the hotel, they would comment that they were kind of worried. I was in a weird situation being torn between a place where people were establishing a relationship with me, but wanting more room, more stability and a feeling of permanence. Maslow's hierarchy of needs says psychological needs are the foundation of the pyramid. I had air and water. My food and sleep needs were met. I had shelter but not in a safe or secure manner. My foundation was pretty solid but my second section of my pyramid was under construction. The second section is Safety needs. I had a roof and a locked room, but going through the prices changing so erratically, I was not feeling very safe. An increased price could put me on the streets. With the scare from before I started my search again for an apartment. I had been in contact with a local resource to help me with my limitations in certain areas. They assigned me a really nice case manager who was able to help me in the areas where I was lacking. When I asked him how he could help, he basically reassured me that I would be moving into my own place soon. I was hopeful, but much like my experience with the employment services, I was very excited and also severely disappointed. I just needed someone with a direct connection to a landlord to discuss with them my predicament. My experience in housing reminded me that the best way to avoid fair housing violations was to remove emotions from the application acceptance process. While the violation may not be intentional, if you accept an application for someone that has a blemish that you denied someone else for, it can be twisted. I tried to not be angry at all of the denials I received, but it was difficult when I knew I was not necessarily the reason for whatever the denial would be for. I could explain all of it. I just wanted someone to talk to about my situation. I was directed to an apartment that had subsidized housing and I wanted to live there so badly. It was pretty centrally located. Downstairs was a cafe, a restaurant and a bar. I was so excited. The building had an elevator and I was able to get around easily. And was within my price range. Unfortunately, they too were terribly disappointing. Even though they were an apartment that was there for those that need subsidized housing, they weren't tolerant of the situations that put a person in the situation to need that type of housing. I got a denial from them and again, no way to explain the reasons for their denial. I asked several people to help as a cosigner, everyone I asked just made excuses. It hurt, but I remembered that I was the only one fighting this fight for me.

This is when I thought I would start looking at other options. My online activity led me to activism. I felt like I was in a situation where traditional options for housing weren't working for me. Necessity is the mother of invention. My invention was to create my own solution. If traditional housing wasn't working, then I would venture out and expand my options. I thought about how many other people were not able to get into housing because of a major medical event destroying their credit, their income and their rental histories. A long night of brainstorming and HouseABLE was born. It is only a brain child at the moment, but It will forever remain a philanthropic endeavor of mine. HouseABLE is going to be a proactive solution to help people at risk of losing their housing, or dealing with involuntary houselessness. No one should ever have to hear "You basically aren't homeless enough for help!" ever again.

Within my first couple months in the hotel I found an apartment complex that had an opening for me, as long as I could get approved for rental assistance. I contacted my local housing assistance resource and went through their application process. I waited weeks and weeks for a response. All the while preparing for a potential move out of the hotel. This was excellent timing, because I saved most of my initial lump sum payment from disability. I finally got fed up with the waiting and I decided that I wanted to be a thorn in their side and I would start calling regularly until a decision is made. That wouldn't be necessary. When I called, they advised me that I was denied assistance. When I asked why, they informed me that it was because I lived in a hotel, I was not considered homeless! *A HOTEL*! This is why society is such a mess. Not because transgender people play sports, but because we live in a reactionary society that believes resorting to living in a hotel out of survival, is not homelessness. You want to focus on improving mental health? Focus on poverty and not keeping people below the poverty line! When people have clean air, clean water, a livable wage, a home and food. Mental health would be much better. This conversation with the representative was when I made the comment that I basically wasn't homelessness enough to receive the help and the representative confirmed and repeated what I said. She even giggled when she repeated it back. It turned my stomach, I was disgusted. Once again, my ability to land on my feet was enough to put me outside the range to be eligible for assistance.

I was tired of constantly being held down in this world. My credit score was never good enough, my resume was never good enough, I never had enough status. I have always heard that necessity is the mother of invention. I decided to create my own solution. I imagined how many other people were experiencing involuntary homelessness that needed a hand up. In the hotel, I met a lot of people that fell on hard times and needed a place like the extended stay hotel. While I was there, I met a woman who had major health issues and her and her husband were both on a fixed income. She walked around on a rollater with no front wheels on it. They were easily some of the most vulnerable of the vulnerable and it was so disheartening to listen to what this world has put them through. The scammers, the evictions, the broken promises and the rugs that had been pulled from under them. I don't know how much of it was on them, but I do know there is always a little accountability in all of those situations. The difference is I didn't judge them for what I assumed. The sad thing is that I bet that they voted for Trump, they had that vibe, to be honest. They seemed like the type that would vote against their own best interests because they didn't want another black president. The thing about me, is even though I would be irritated to find out that they would be willing to vote against their own best interest, I still wouldn't be ok with them living like this. In a proactive world, we recognize that issues can arise for many different reasons. Getting ahead of those reasons can stop the domino from falling into the next. Instead of picking up the dominos after the damage is done, try getting ahead of the first domino that would cause a chain reaction in the first place.

Focusing on proactive measures, we could work towards ending involuntary homelessness. Involuntary homelessness happens in a number of ways and I had brainstormed a number of solutions for those problems. I took a few days and this was my sole purpose. I thought about not only housing, but food, water, air and any of the human essentials. But through my brainstorming and solution based thinking, I birthed HouseABLE. I was literally experiencing a crisis that I referred to as being unhouseable. I tried to pull in the media, just to bring this issue to the light. I woke up some mornings from the sound of a school bus picking up students that were living in the hotel. That is a problem. Children do not deserve to not have their own bed, or their own room. Everyday, my empathetic heart ached knowing that whichever children were being picked up for school were likely being bullied or there are kids that are spreading that information to people that are bullying them. By some wild stroke of luck I hoped that Kelly Clarkson, Jennifer Hudson, Drew Barrymore, Sherri Shepard or the Fab Five would see my letter and want to reach out to me about helping a disabled person, to help with housing. I know that my story was marketable and could be sold very easily. My experience on social media had proven that people looking for that kind of story seemed to like it. I tried reaching out to the daytime talkshows that love those stories, I tried reaching out to major news media outlets. I even reached out to local media in the hopes that it would grab the attention of other media. I knew that people didn't care enough about homelessness to end it. Nearly any billionaire in this country could end homelessness and still be a billionaire. The same with hunger and food disparities. If they cared they could end it and I'm certain they wouldn't care about a disabled, transgender, latina being houseless, but maybe I could get a crowd of people to listen. If not a crowd, then maybe the microphone would be powerful enough to shine the light on a bigger issue that seems to be ignored.

The letters that I sent were not long, but they were powerful, explanatory and came with a call to action. I was hopeful, but I know that the people I was reaching out to had an agenda of their own. They wanted a story that would sell. They cared about ratings. I cared about having a home. They wouldn't care that I was trauma bonded to my last apartment. I was living in my childhood home, I had just suffered a small stroke, unbeknownst to me at the time. My mother was asking everyday, when I was leaving. Getting approved for my apartment with no help from anyone was so empowering. That apartment was a savior for me at that time. The want the tears and the emotional reactions. But I still wanted to try.

Here is a copy of the letters I sent.

To whom this story would be of interest,

I hope this message finds you well. My name is Meetri'a Angelo, and I am reaching out to share an important story that I believe would resonate with your audience. I have attached the full story with all of the details. The summary is this. I am 38, I suffered a major stroke, lost everything during my recovery and since being out of the nursing/rehab facility. I'm fighting for housing and have been officially homeless for over a year.

Given your commitment to covering impactful stories, I would love the opportunity to discuss this further and explore how we could collaborate to bring this to light. I believe your platform is an ideal place for this conversation to unfold.

Thank you for considering this request. I look forward to the possibility of working together to inform and engage your readership.

Meetri'a Angelo

I felt unhouseable with societal standards in the housing industry. It was rough because I was fighting an uphill battle. Between the current housing situation in this country and Trump taking office bragging about wanting to deregulate housing, I was terrified that I may never be out of the hotel. I had a plan and I had a purpose now I needed the means. Money! I was going to apply for a 501c3 non-profit status, because I wanted the houseABLE program to be non-profit. I want the revenue that is not paying for employees to go back into the program. I have visions of apartments, extended stay hotels, both of which have employment needs, which could be filled by people in the program experiencing job loss or other employment issues. I imagine programs around financial literacy. Resume building, job placement. I have so many things. The idea is to save the housing that people are currently in as long as it is affordable, necessary and manageable. I also want an option for those who have already lost their housing and need to get back into permanent housing. Starter money is not something that comes around easily. In order for you to obtain funds from non-profit grants you need years of your non-profit operation to show. I didn't want years more in the hotel, so I looked for other options. Something I've found on TikTok was that crowdsourcing on a livestream was a thing. It was interesting because it was kind of like QVC Fundraising. The product was contributing to someone you believe is doing a good thing. It required a little entertainment and a large crowd, but it was possible. I have watched it happen. I watched people raise hundreds of dollars just for simply being the creator that they liked. I've watched a crowd of people raise money for veterans, when Trump started cutting funding. I watched crowd sourcing for many reasons. I saw an out. I saw a way to get out of the hotel. Having my experience in housing, I know that one way to avoid a denial from credit or income is to have the full lease amount upfront. This was unreasonable for someone receiving barely $2,000 a month and anywhere from 50-75% of it was being used to live in a hotel. It could be possible with some crowd funding. Around this time, I went to go pay for another month at the hotel and when I went to the front desk, I saw a face I recognized. A CNA that I met in the nursing home was in the hotel lobby. Our history was complicated. We spent time together outside of the nursing home. We went to garage sales, she drove me to a speaking event on trans rights. Shortly after Kamala Harris announced her run, she showed the truth behind her friendly smile. She was a victim of the patriarchy, believing that women need men and a vile Trump supporter. She saw nothing wrong with disparaging transgender children and spreading harmful rhetoric. She also acknowledged she was a Trump supporter. I made a vow to not have Trump supporters in my life. It's not about a vote, it's about their morals. If you voted for a man accused of rape and a man listed in the Epstein files more times than Harry Potter is named in all seven books. You either have no morals that I care to be around or you like his atrocities against humanity.

Seeing the real her behind the curtain was disappointing, but her role in this chapter of my story was actually great. She was friendly and we talked for a while and we caught up. She had her apartment sold out from underneath her and she was at the hotel temporarily. I continued my participation in TikTok panels and got more educated on politics. I continued hosting lives and establishing relationships. I treated them all as genuine relationships, but I made it a point to remember that it may be para social. Maybe I had a bond that I felt for them but online bonds gave people a reason to never become fully attached. I think this is another reason that the other women, in my group that I quickly found myself in, were so easily able to walk away from me the way they did. Either way, my online presence grew. Randomly, I ran into my former CNA and she told me that she got into a new place. I probed her on it and got some information. She said that she was shocked that they accepted her, because her credit was not that great. This told me, as a former property manager, that maybe the complex had low occupancy. When occupancy falls below 80% the management company is typically willing to compromise on their requirements for leasing. I reached out and I spoke with a leasing agent that was so kind and understanding. She listened to me. It was different though. She sounded sincere. She sounded like she truly cared about my situation. I actually felt it. The application fee was higher than most, but I figured that I wont know if i'd get in without applying.

I submitted the application and followed up when I needed to. I had gotten through sending in my documents and all of that. I was trying to not get my hopes up, but I remained optimistic. A new month was approaching and I was getting uneasy about my money. With paying for my hotel and then maybe having to shell out tons of money for my new apartment I wasn't sure that I would have enough to pay for both and typically an apartment complex will not hold the apartment for you for longer than a few weeks. I wouldn't afford to be able to lose the apartment that they had for me. They had a first floor unit. No stairs. It was great for me. The property was beautiful and the people were so incredibly nice. I really didn't want to lose this space. I was working on my schoolwork one afternoon when I heard my phone ring. I saw the number and recognized that it was the apartment complex. I knew that I could be denied and I didn't want to get hurt again. I hesitantly answered.

"Hey Meetri'a, we got your result back from our regional." She said calmly and even cheery as I braced for the impact of continued disappointment.

I have been fighting a place back in the real world since

December 2024. I convinced myself to get back in the job market, just to get housing, I applied to government programs, I lost friends and family simply asking for help to have a place to live. It was a long long road of negatives and no's. I was trying to act calm as she continued.

"You've been approved! The unit will be ready within the next week." Wait! Did she just say yes?

Everything went quiet. For a moment I only heard the faint humming of the room lighting. Only when the first tear fell did the sound return.

"Are you there?" she asked because of the silence on my end.

"Yes! I'm sorry! So, I was approved?" I asked, at this point I didn't know if I was imagining that.

"Yes I did. Are you okay?" After she said 'yes I did', I must have whimpered or something, she knew I was crying.

I literally felt years of bad emotions just wash away. Everything that was fighting me in this world suddenly felt like it couldn't hurt me anymore, let alone break me. I was approved for a year-long lease, not a month to month at a hotel that could throw away everything that I worked for into the dumpster again. I was taken back to when my mother declined to help and I still landed on my feet. I did it on my own, well mostly, I'll talk about that in a moment. I got the dates figured out and the move in costs. I was grounded really quickly when the number $2500 came up for move-in costs. As quickly as I pictured my new future and my new life, was how quickly it vanished. Where in the fuck was I going to get that kind of money? One of the people I followed on TikTok when I first got on the app, she offered to hold a fundraiser for me. I always had trouble asking for help. Especially after my mother used those vulnerable moments to make me feel like a failure. I also struggled with accepting the gifts that were offered to me, on the rare occasions I was offered anything. The day came that my fundraiser was going to happen. Part of me was hopeful, but part of me wondered if this was a time for watching everything fall apart all over again. I set my accounts up in the linktree in my bio on my profile and I prepared my story for anyone that would want to hear it. As the time grew near, my anxiety was reeving up. This was my only chance for me to pay for this opportunity.

The time finally came and I was brought up immediately. I told my story from the beginning. I spoke of my stroke, my recovery in the nursing home, my loss of everything, I spoke of my stay in the hotel and how it lacked being a home. I answered questions. I was naked and vulnerable to like 500 people. My phone dinged a few times with some small donations and I was nervous that I was headed for another heartbreak. When I started resigning to the fact that people were probably not going to find my story interesting enough for me to get the help I needed was that moment that I realized that my vulnerability was worth it. The next thing I knew my phone notifications couldn't come in fast enough. I thought that my phone was actually going to explode. The donations were rolling in. Some small, some large! I was absolutely speechless. In a few minutes all of the voices that told me I wasn't deserving were all silenced. I was helpful in so many ways. People finally listened to me. The apartment complex heard my plea just for a chance and granted me one. These kind people heard my story and wanted to help. My mother had the opportunity to help with her signature and she told me that I wasn't worthy enough. My brothers were, but I wasn't. These people were coming off of their hard earned cash! It was a huge shift in my self worth. At the end of the day I had enough generosity come my way that I had enough to pay the move-in costs but I was also able to lightly furnish it. All of the belongings were thrown out. Whatever my brother was able to get out of my apartment was stuck in my mother's basement, likely collecting mold or mildew, they never took care of their wet basement and I wasn't willing to compromise my peace away from the toxicity to collect some mildewy clothes from a damp basement I knew all too well. I decided to spend smartly and refurnish my life with the generosity I was given.

I signed my lease the next day and paid my move-in costs. It felt surreal that I would only be in the hotel for another week. I made some online purchases like a bed frame and a mattress in a box. I just needed a bed for the most part. I didn't care what else I had, as long as I had a proper bed to sleep in. The rest could come later. I packed the hotel room, which seemed like so much compared to what I came with. I had been living there for 22 months. I collected a lot. My chosen family helped me move from the hotel to my new apartment. I didn't ask them to, but they helped me put my bed together, too. I never looked back at the hotel again.

I had proven that I was houseABLE. It was such a full feeling. I felt complete. I moved in on October 7th, 2025 and I have been through so much, but also nothing that I haven't been prepared for. Hind sight is always 20/20 but I went through so many things before that prepared me for things that have happened. I've made some decisions that have proven to be likely for the best. I have limited my alcohol intake to roughly once per month in a brunch setting. This has been a good balance for socializing and partaking in alcohol without a huge impact on my health. I have taken my ride service much more rather than asking my friends for rides or to transport my wheelchair. This has been better on my relationships and it's been better on me feeling like I am less of a burden. I started relying more on my ride service before leaving the hotel. Pride 2025 was much different than the year before, because of my surge of independence.

My ride service transports me in my wheelchair and it makes it much easier for me to get around stores or festivals like Pride. I was dropped off right at the entrance and I took my charger but I didn't have to plug in to charge at all. I was there for 6 hours and then was picked up where I was dropped off. Easy there, easy back. I missed the after party at my chosen family's pop up bar, but I wasn't missing much. At least I don't feel like I did. I didn't need the booze, I didn't need the bar tab, I didn't need to watch everyone else dance the night away while I was in my chair. Pride 2025 was so different from the year before. I was left to my own devices, in the best way possible. I still hung out with people. I still got to shop at some local vendors. I got to reconnect with some people that I hadn't seen in awhile.

Since living in my new home. I have continued my growth and recovery from my stroke. I am still wheelchair dependent, but I am working on that too. My other growth has been in the form of pursuing my master's degree in counseling. I am planning to use that degree to help people with family trauma, LGBTQ clients, Medical grief trauma and other mental health barriers people are experiencing. I also found the motivation to continue my writing endeavors. I actually met a guy on TikTok that found out that I had written and published 'A Stroke of Recovery'. He thought it was awesome and like a cheerleader, he told everyone that joined his livestreams. He really started a resurgence of my first book. This really got me excited to finish this one and continue. I always predicted that my first book would give me the knowledge and connections. I predicted my second book would be the breakthrough book that would open the right doors. Then I predicted that my third book would be the one that really changed my career. That was the plan. I always wished that my first book would explode, but I'm a realist. I was never someone that had the luck to just fall into success. I was excited to finish my first book, this book was started immediately after my first one was finished. As life does, my focus was pulled elsewhere and I forgot to continue writing. I just lived life. I was still not focused on writing even after getting into my new apartment. It wasn't until someone I barely knew, from an online friendship, created a surge of energy around my first book. I sat down and told myself, it was time to finish the follow-up. I wanted the second book to be Part 2: Recovery Completed. As I said earlier, recovery is not something that always has a finish line. For some people the recovery is something that continues the rest of your life. When I first had my stroke, I looked up a lot of stroke stories for inspiration. I found one story of a doctor that finally regained full control of his stroke affected side over 20 years after his stroke. I am beginning to feel like that may be the case for me. I remind myself everyday that every little move or twitch in my finger could mean movement soon. Every pain in my foot could be my neural pathways reconnecting. You never know until you know. Either way, I am finally out of the hotel. I am years out from my stroke and my stint in the nursing home. During a conversation with my case manager I was explaining my need for my own home. I reminded him that I had a bachelors degree in business and a certificate in small business sitting in their beautiful frames. They were wrapped up in a drawer. I wanted to hang my college degrees on my wall, in my home. This wasn't just a selfish want. Everyday that I wake up in my home and look at those degrees I am reminded of my entire life. I am reminded that I was born and quickly lost my biological father in months. My mother and I lived alone, struggling for years, but we made it. She met the man that would later molest me. I moved away from my first best friend and my adaptive grandparents across the street when I was six. I was molested at 10 and tortured by that man for decades after. My story should have landed me on the street, on drugs and/or dead at a very young age. I graduated high school and chose to work. I wasn't able to be funded for college. Two years after I graduated, the city I live in came out with The Kalamazoo Promise which sent graduates to college for 4 years in Michigan. I was working great jobs making a lot of money but still wanted a college degree. I started school in 2019 and finally finished my bachelor's degree at the University of Phoenix in 2024. I have started pursuing my Master's in 2025. I have published two books and I'm working on a third. So much has been a hurdle for me to overcome, but I have cleared so many of them even with people praying that I'd trip up. My name has legally changed and in my life, I will live unapologetically myself as a protest to the bigots and the haters. It is a great feeling to know that I didn't follow through with a permanent solution to a temporary problem. I have so many things that I could be worried about but I continue to press forward and I won't let my past dictate my future. My struggles helped to shape me but they do not define me. As I write this today, I have experienced a very emotionally charged week. I decided to go live and talk to my community. I spent most of the time telling my story, in search of a pity party, but I was grounded by one of my followers.

She said "Tomorrow will be better." posting in my chat.

She was right. That weekend I had a nail appointment, a political town hall to attend and then I had drag bingo. So I was hoping for a better weekend. It struck me funny. I spend my days getting online and inspiring people to keep fighting for their livelihood, especially in this political environment. Ironically, today I needed the boost. I needed the reminder that I needed to continue to move forward. She reminded me that one bad day doesn't mean a bad life. It was a great reminder that even the one who lifts people up sometimes needs a lift. It was nice to see that the community that I've been trying to build, spreading positivity and helping me in return. I felt a full circle moment, that read like an accomplishment to me. I wrote my first book to spread awareness and positivity, I started on social media to spread positivity. I wrote this book for the same reason and that awareness and positivity was boomeranged back at me.

The next days were better! I met some new people, made some networking connections and It was a great weekend. I needed the reminder that that tough times don't last forever. The down days always feel like they lasted for an eternity and then a good day comes and everything seems miles behind you. That is what I equate the Trump presidency and the MAGA blood cult to. They are a temporary bad day. Better days are ahead. 10 years is a long, bad, day. However they are temporary. It took 100 years for them to implement their racist Jim Crow laws. It took another 60 years for them to pack the courts, find enough loyalists and emerge from hiding to expose all of their racism, bigotry and misogyny, but they aren't permanent. The bad days aren't permanent.

As my bad day lifted and June approached, I started feeling my pride kick in. I had been considering a permanent name change for a long time. I recently went to a name change workshop and I was running an errand to get the process started and decided to visit a local Starbucks. I wheeled in and in the corner of the shop I saw my sister in law. I had been no contact with her and the family for two years now. I had been missing them and even talking about them in therapy. I don't know if it was the universe, if it was our energies attracting each other or just pure circumstance, but we were both in the same room suddenly. I felt my heart rate pick up and I knew that this situation could end in an interaction. It wasn't bad, but it could be difficult because she was a person that I ended communication with because of her proximity to my mother and brother and truthfully, I didn't want her to catch strays for remaining in contact with me while they were shut out. Several things rushed through my mind about what could happen here. Since my stroke, my emotions have been severely intensified. I cry from the smallest things. I knew there would be emotions, but I didn't know if they would be manageable or if I would be inconsolable. Either way, this was going to be something big.

I sat there editing this book and soon, her meeting ended and I braced myself for whatever would happen. As her colleague left I saw her coming towards me. She came over and immediately extended for a hug. I burst into tears. She said she has been thinking about me and the kids still ask about me. The tears continued down my face and then she updated me about her, the kids and my dog. Her dad took Appa in. He is happy, in a home with someone who loves him and he is spoiled. Recently she sent me a photo of him in a food coma after he was fed a sub sandwich. It was hilarious. I gave her my number and we hugged and she left. We have been in contact since and I believe this is the start of a reunion. It may not be with the entire family, but at least with the ones that will understand me the most. The future holds great things.

Shortly after, I received a letter that said that my name change petition was approved. During a year of exaggerated rhetoric and egregious bigotry, When trans people were named as a terrorist group, the "president" even threatened us on a national scale. In a time filled with unfounded hate and unwarranted fear, I resisted it all and in the face of adversity I chose to process a legal name change. There were rumors within the community that these were the things that could get you on a 'list'. The book On Tyranny by Timothy Snyder says the first rule of fighting tyranny is to not comply in advance. Showing the fear mongering thugs that you are willing to give up without a fight, is like walking them to victory. Even in my weakened state, I will not just bow down to this. When we are on the other side of this, we will realize that every bit of resistance to this helped. The way that every new atrocity feels like another unbearable obstacle. Every pride festival, every affirmed trans person, every progressive win adds more weight to their shoulders. W need to continue to hold the pressure.

I had an idea that completing the foundation of my needs pyramid would make building my life easier. Life isn't gravy, but I have so many less stressers than before. My growth since January 13, 2023 has been huge and my stroke exposed what I had, what I lost and what I've taken for granted. My stroke took so many things from me, but has also paved the way for so much more. My stroke hit me when I didn't care if I was going to live or die and it gave me countless reasons to live. Everything that I have gained from this stroke continues to pave my road of recovery and my current situation has me in a great position to continue my growth. My current situation also gives me the opportunity to put a bookmark in this story and focus on something different for a while. As I put this book down for awhile I will never forget that while I focused on destroying my life, my stroke came in to help me recover to where I am now. I am forever thankful that I understood that this was a stroke of recovery.

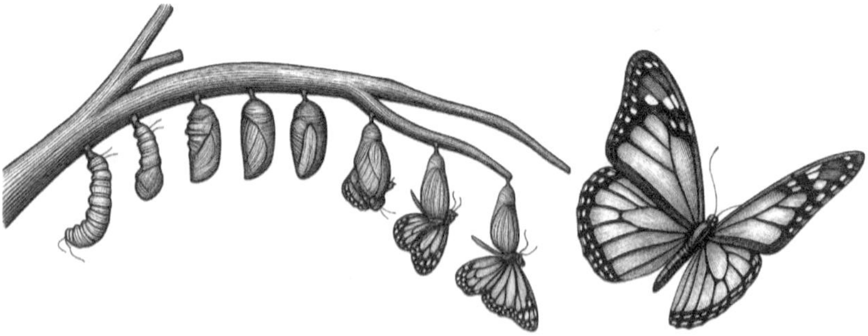

www.ingramcontent.com/pod-product-compliance
Lightning Source LLC
LaVergne TN
LVHW092136071126
851857LV00038BB/462
* 9 7 9 8 9 9 6 1 9 7 5 1 4 *